A BOAT
IN OUR
BAGGAGE

A BOAT IN OUR BAGGAGE

Around the World with a Kayak

Maria Coffey

Photographs by
Dag Goering

Ragged Mountain Press
Camden, Maine

For Bee and Justina

Published by Ragged Mountain Press

10 9 8 7 6 5 4 3 2 1

First Published in Great Britain in 1994 by Little, Brown
Abacus Travel edition published in Great Britain in 1995

Printed in the United States of America.

Library of Congress Cataloging-in-Publication Data

Coffey, Maria. 1952–
 A boat in our baggage : around the world with a kayak / Maria
Coffey : photographs by Dag Goering.
  p. cm.
 Includes index.
 ISBN 0-07-011547-8
 1. Coffey, Maria, 1952– . 2. Goering, Dag. 3. Canoeist–
–Biography. 4. Women Canoeists—Biography. 5. Sea kayaking.
6. Voyages around the world. I. Title
GV782.42.C64A3 1995
797.1'23'092—dc20
 [B] 95–3117
 CIP

Questions regarding the content of this book should be addressed to:
Ragged Mountain Press
P.O. Box 220
Camden, ME 04843

Questions regarding the ordering of this book should be addressed to:
The McGraw-Hill Companies
Customer Service Department
P.O. Box 547
Blacklick, OH 43004
Retail customers: 1-800-822-8158
Bookstores: 1-800-722-4726

A portion of the profits from the sale of each Ragged Mountain Press book
is donated to an environmental cause.

✪ *A Boat in Our Baggage* is printed on 45-pound Editor's Eggshell

Printed by R. R. Donnelley & Sons, Crawfordsville, IN
Design by Ken Gross
Production by Dan Kirchoff

Contents

Acknowledgments

Our venture was greatly helped by the companies who so generously sponsored us, and we wish to thank:

Feathercraft Products Ltd. for the boat in our baggage; Qantas Airlines for transporting the baggage free of charge; Dermtek Pharmaceuticals for the Ombrelle sun lotion and the unexpected financial gift; The New Delhi Maurya Sheraton Hotel for its supreme comfort and its unsurpassable chocolate mousse; Lisle Kelco Ltd. for the tough cases which not only protected Dag's cameras but also served as chopping boards and seats; Cascade Designs Inc. for the waterproof Great Barrier bags; Mustang Manufacturing for the Meta Inflatable Collars; Tilley Endurables Inc. for the hats and clothes; Berghaus for the rucksacks and sweaters; ACR Electronics Inc. for the emergency locator unit and Firefly strobes which thankfully we never had to use; Moss Tents for our Deltoid tent; Teva and Nike Inc. for our footwear; Powerfood Inc. for the delicious Powerbars; Georgia Bay Kayak Ltd. for the sea anchor; Parlour Products Plc. for the Mosquito Milk; Dr. Stan Eng, Ciba Vision and Alcon Canada Inc. for my contact lenses and solutions; Geodicke und Co. for the Ewa Marine chart covers which kept our maps dry.

Just as it has been impossible for me to record in one book all we experienced during our journey, so I am unable to list everyone who helped us and offered us hospitality along the way. Many of these people are mentioned in the text; in the chapters on

Malawi, I have changed most of their names. Our heartfelt thanks go to them all—they left us with a renewed faith in the essential goodness of mankind.

We especially wish to thank Jurgen Goering for looking after our affairs in Canada; Bapi Sarkar for his songs, laughter and enthusiasm; and Lord and Lady Wilson, Maria Osmon, Shona Adhikari, Olaf Fiegel, Sabine Zuschrott and my family for their warm welcomes and the much appreciated homes away from home they provided.

For their practical help and advice we are grateful to: The South Pacific Peoples Foundation of Canada, the members of CUSO we met on Saltspring Island, Clark Stede and Michelle Poncini, Gord Hartman, Tony Gibb and Connie McCann, John Dowd, Avinash Koli, Colonel Kumar, Sudhi Sahi, Tejbir and Mala Singh, Tarana Maya Das, Mr. J. D. Gupta, Reg Noble, Cindy Pilskaln, Sharon and Dennis Tweddle.

For their part in the creation of this book, I am indebted to my agent, Vivienne Schuster; Hilary Foakes of Little, Brown and Company; and my computer guardian angel, Liz Hammond-Kaarremaa.

Most of all, my love and thanks to Dag, for having the idea in the first place, and for his indefatigable sense of humor that kept me laughing all the way around the world.

A BOAT IN OUR BAGGAGE

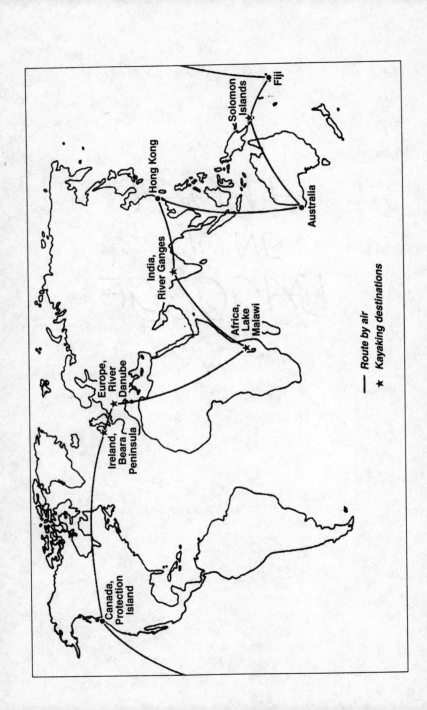

Route by air

★ Kayaking destinations

Fiji

Solomon Islands

Hong Kong

Australia

India, River Ganges

Africa, Lake Malawi

Europe, River Danube

Ireland, Beara Peninsula

Canada, Protection Island

1

A Daunting Prospect

Fine red desert dust streamed through holes in the floor of the taxi. Every warning light was on, and where once had been seat belt mountings were two large stereo speakers blasting out Mexican pop music. The driver's head bobbed about in time with the songs, and as he took a corner on two wheels, a statuette of the Virgin Mary hanging from the rearview mirror swung crazily from side to side.

Next to me on the back seat, Dag was staring out of the window with a glazed expression on his face, as if he wasn't seeing the scrub desert landscape flying by. I, however, was gripped with terror. When the Virgin Mary started to pirouette, I could stand no more.

"Slow down!" I yelled at the driver, who obediently reached for a knob on the radio, dropping the music level enough for us to hear the squealing of the tires.

"OK, señora, OK, I turn it down," he said, grinning devilishly at me in the mirror. "You no like Mexican songs?"

Sitting back, I resigned myself to my fate. It was at least six more miles to Loreto, from where we were to catch a plane that afternoon.

"I hated packing up the boat," sighed Dag.

He was referring to the folding kayak we had just taken apart and stuffed into the trunk of the taxi. It was an ingenious, sea-worthy craft, big enough for us, our camping gear and a good supply of food and water. We had spent the last three weeks paddling it on Mexico's Sea of Cortez, where we'd faced stiff winds and steep seas, but nothing as alarming as this taxi ride.

"I felt as if I was just getting into my stride," he said. "I could have carried on for months."

We were now on a long, straight and narrow stretch of road. On one side of us was a sheer sandstone cliff, on the other a rutted and cactus-covered plain. Ahead, through a cloud of dust, a local bus was approaching. As it drew nearer, I realized we were on a collision course. Both drivers were hunched over their steering wheels, with no obvious intention of giving way or even slowing down. A game of chicken was being enacted, with us and a full contingent of bus passengers its hapless victims.

"I've just had an idea!" cried Dag.

The bus was now so close that I could see the alarmed expressions of its passengers.

"Let's quit work for a year," he continued, apparently oblivious to our imminent death, "and go kayaking all over the world!"

Moments before impact, the two drivers swung their respective steering wheels—luckily in opposite directions. We scraped along the side of the cliff while the bus careered across ruts and between cactus trees before regaining the road. The sudden movement threw me heavily against Dag, who took this to be a sign of agreement and gleefully hugged me.

"We'll start planning as soon as we get home!" he announced.

An exact definition of "home" was tricky for us, as our roots were widely spread. For the last few years, its nearest approximation had been the west coast of Canada. We met there in 1986, when I was over from England to work as an exchange teacher and Dag had come from Germany to do his Ph.D. research. At the end of that year, I should have been back in Manchester, and Dag in Munich. Instead, we were living together on tiny Protection Island, a mile and a half from the far bigger Vancouver Island. I was writing a book, and Dag was trying to boost his dwindling research fund by working part-time in a friend's fiberglass shop. It was there that Dag got one of his ideas: to build two kayaks so that we could cheaply commute between Protection Island and Nanaimo, the nearest town. I wasn't exactly enthusiastic about this plan. I barely knew what a kayak looked like, but had vague memories from school geography lessons of fur-wrapped Eskimos in flimsy sealskin boats. The prospect of paddling my groceries home wasn't an appealing one, and I railed against it until the day Dag introduced me to the new kayaks. They bore no resemblance to the ones I'd seen in school geography books. They were fourteen feet long, pointed at either end and fat in the middle. Each had a cockpit fitted with a comfortable bucket seat and foot pedals to work the rudder. Awkwardly, I clambered into mine and tentatively paddled along Protection Island's rocky shoreline. A great blue heron hunkered on the beach, undisturbed by my quiet progress, and a curious seal surfaced so close to me that I could almost touch its nose. As I paddled away from the shelter of the shore, a wave rushed toward me, its top curling into a white crest. I stiffened, but the wave passed beneath the kayak and I was lifted and set down again like a piece of driftwood. Eagerly I paddled on, enjoying the wind on my face, the rhythmic movement, the sense of being part of the ocean. I didn't know it then, but I was hooked.

From the beginning, kayaking for us was more a means of transportation than a sport. Initially it was how we got ourselves and our shopping between town and home, then it became a way of exploring the world around us. We went off for weeks on end, meandering up and down the coastline of British Columbia. Our boats drew only a few inches of water, and we were therefore able to access beaches and bays unsuitable for most other craft. We could carry enough gear, food and water to be totally self-sufficient. As it was impossible for us to do more than a few knots an hour, we had lots of time to see clouds form and dissolve, to watch the patterns made when wind meets water, to observe animals and birds. The more we paddled, the farther we wanted to go. When we got married, my parents wrote us out a hefty check and told us to use it for something that would make us happy. We bought a double folding kayak and headed down to Mexico.

During that dreadful taxi ride, the idea of a year-long, worldwide kayak trip had seemed quite feasible. Back in our cozy home, however, it was a daunting prospect. Night after night, Dag pored over the atlas, muttering ominous place names: "the Zaire River . . . the Andaman Islands . . . Mongolia . . . . "

He wanted, he told me, to go to some remote corners of the

world, places that weren't easy to reach. The more I thought about the logistics of this proposed trip, the more disquieting they became.

"What if one of us gets sick?" I nervously inquired, imagining tropical terrors like worms crawling across my eyeballs and larvae burrowing into my skin. "What about wild animals?" I continued. "And bandits and riptides and storms?"

But Dag was born with a sunny optimism which his thirty-six years had left untainted. "Remember that taxi ride in Mexico?" he asked. "And how dangerous it was?"

I certainly did.

"We'll avoid taxis!" he pronounced, and returned to the atlas.

There was, I had to admit, a growing sense of inevitability about this venture. During the previous four years we had established careers, bought land on Protection Island, built a house and planted a garden. The next logical step, so the people around us intimated, was to start a family and prepare for a comfortable, secure middle age. But our restless spirits weren't having any of this. They began tugging at our roots, whispering to us to glance up from our safe little world and out to the much bigger and uncertain one beyond. Dag was easily convinced, but I equivocated. The coward in me argued with the restless spirit, and came up with all sorts of excuses for staying put.

"That house you've built isn't finished," the coward insisted. "Look, it hasn't even got any drainpipes from the gutters yet."

"Drainpipes!" snorted Dag, when I relayed this to him one night. "Who cares about *drainpipes*?"

His roots were already out of the ground and trailing along behind him. I had the options of yanking mine up as well, or staying at home and worrying about drainpipes. In the end, it wasn't a difficult decision.

Dag arranged for a year's leave of absence from his college job, and I found myself discussing "our trip," and the book I'd write about it, with everyone I met. Unconsciously, I was using a ploy, a type of self-daring, that I had developed long ago: talking so freely about my ambitions that eventually I felt duty-bound to turn them into reality. At the New Year's Eve party we threw to herald 1991, at least half of our guests asked us when we were leaving on "our trip." When the first hangovers of the year had subsided, we began serious planning.

For months we discussed, researched and argued over the itinerary, then made our final decisions in a capricious fashion. We read up on the South Pacific and found tourist information on everywhere except the Solomon Islands, so decided that was the place for us. Inspired by Eric Newby's *Slowly Down the Ganges,* I suggested we kayak along India's holiest river. At a conference, Dag met an Englishman who worked in Malawi and who fired him up with tales of that country's marvelous lake. Wanting to visit friends and family in Europe, we slotted a trip along the River Danube into the grand plan, and to round things off we decided on a final jaunt in Alaska. We sat back and congratulated each other for a job well done. Then the nasty subject of money cropped up.

One evening in February 1991, we realized that our finances and the estimated cost of our trip were two sides of an unbalanced equation. As well as travel and living expenses, we were going to need a new boat and equipment of high enough quality to sustain months of continuous hard wear in a variety of climates and conditions. Quite simply, we didn't have enough money for everything. As this unpleasant fact sank in, we sat in glum silence. I don't know what Dag's thoughts were, but I was casting my mind back to my life in England, which for ten years had been linked through friendships and romance to the British mountaineering scene. I'd witnessed the preparations for numerous climbing expeditions to the Himalayas, I'd listened to phone calls to arrange last-minute monetary and product sponsorship, and I'd seen mounds of new, donated gear grow on living-room floors.

"Let's go for sponsorship," I suggested to Dag.

He gave me a blank look. "Why would anyone sponsor us?"

"Why wouldn't they? How many people have spent a year kayaking in different parts of the world? We'll call ourselves an expedition . . . ."

My voice trailed off as I realized that, yet again, I was dragging out the old self-daring ploy.

"It's a brilliant idea," he said, in an awestruck tone. "You're in charge. You tell me what to do."

At the time, I was teaching English as a Second Language to recent immigrants to Canada. One day, a guest speaker came to give my class a talk entitled "Starting a New Business." Ann, a buxom woman in her early thirties, spent most of her allotted hour discussing different ways of raising capital. Over coffee, I told her of our impending trip and my sponsorship idea.

"Companies will be lining up to back you!" she cried. "They'll pay for everything, they'll even give you a salary on top of expenses. Why don't you let me help you? I'd love to be involved."

I rushed home to share the good news with Dag, who was immediately infected by my enthusiasm. The next afternoon, we met Ann in a wine bar. Between conversations on her cellular phone, she managed to convince us that we should target North America's top companies. As chance would have it, she had a list of these companies, with stock market reports on each, in her briefcase. First, with her help, we would put together a proposal to send to chief executive officers.

"Make it glossy and sensational," she advised. "Photos, maps, information about the countries you're going to and the dangers you'll face. We'll meet again on Monday. Have a first draft ready to show me."

Her phone rang again, and the person on the line summoned her to another meeting.

"Most consultants charge at least $250 a day," she said as she was leaving. "But I like you guys, I'm inspired by what you're doing. I'll settle on 10 percent of whatever sponsorship you get."

After a few more drinks, we weaved our way back to the kayaks. "I don't know about all this," muttered Dag as we paddled home. "It's not our style."

I thought back to Britain, and how the climbers I knew there had raised money. I couldn't recall any snappy, sensational proposals. "This is North America," I said lamely. "It's how things are done here."

The proposal took weeks to prepare. I produced draft after draft to show to Ann. "Not positive enough!" she would say.

She insisted on writing one section, which began: "Ms. Coffey and Dr. Goering represent an ideal couple in that they are young, professional, athletic, attractive and have a real sense of *joie de vivre.*"

"Young?" I asked her. "I'll be turning forty next year."

"Keep the lid on that," she said.

Eventually, we had the finished product. Bound in shiny, laminated plastic, it announced our "Jungle to Ice Expedition" and had an executive overview, chapters on marketing, advertising and promotional strategies, information about our destinations, a detailed budget, and color photographs of us looking like the "ideal couple."

"I don't feel comfortable about all this," I told Dag.

"I said that weeks ago," he replied.

Next, we began contacting companies. The first was American Express.

"I can see it now," said Ann. "A full-page magazine ad of you paddling through shark-infested waters with your credit cards between your teeth."

She gave me the name and number of a top executive. Before I made the phone call, I did deep breathing for ten minutes. Then the number was busy for half an hour. Finally, I got through to the executive's secretary, who demanded to know the nature of my business.

"You need to talk to the director of usage and retention, ma'am," she told me.

"I do?"

"I'll put you through."

The usage and retention man was called Bill, and he was disarmingly self-effacing. "Sounds like I run an incontinence clinic, doesn't it?" he said.

Haltingly, I explained that we were seeking sponsorship for a year-long, worldwide kayaking expedition.

"Fascinating, Maria. Send me a proposal."

The phone went dead. I dialed Ann's number. "I talked to someone at American Express," I told her. "He wants to see a proposal."

"Fantastic!" she screeched. "I knew they'd go for it!"

"He didn't agree to anything . . . "

"Once he sees what you guys have got to offer, he'll go nuts. Now, tell me who he was and *exactly* what you said to him and what he said to you."

She listened. She wasn't pleased.

"You've got to be more assertive than that. You need a conversation flow chart in front of you when you make these calls. You've got to push all the right buttons as soon as you get through."

Before long, our kitchen table was awash with flow charts. By six o'clock each morning we were on the phone to CEOs all over North America. But the more adept we became at pushing buttons, the more we realized that we didn't really want corporate

sponsorship. What we did want, what we'd wanted all along
before we'd been infected by this profit ethic, was an unfettered,
independent adventure.

One day, I was speaking to a promotions officer in New York.
"On my desk right now," he said, "I have a request for funding by
a guy who intends to snowboard down Mount Kilimanjaro,
another from someone who's going to walk across Australia and
back again, and this proposal from you two crazies wanting to
drag a kayak round the world. That's just this week's batch and
it's only Tuesday! How did people like you manage before the
multinationals came along?"

"Listen," I told him. "Take that proposal of ours and throw it in
the paper shredder."

He roared with laughter. "That's the spirit. Have a great trip."

"You want to borrow money for what?"

The loan officer of our bank was a small woman with huge
shoulder pads, lots of costume jewelry and long red fingernails.
Predictably enough, she was unimpressed by our forthcoming
adventure, and her only suggestion was that we request to make a
loan against our mortgage, effectively doubling it, with an interest
rate that made us shudder. We retreated to a nearby café to confer.

"It's an awful lot of money," I mused as cups of coffee were set
down in front of us.

In the long silence that ensued, we both stirred our coffee.
"We could forget the whole idea," said Dag.

I nodded. "That's one possibility." There was another silence
while we drank the coffee.

"Ready?" he asked.

I was. Without further discussion, we returned to the bank and
arranged for a loan.

It was now April, four months before we were due to leave. We
were still on the phone at six o'clock each morning, but now with
the purpose of arranging product sponsorship. Most of the companies we contacted were small, specialized and eager to be
involved with our venture, and we were offered more than we
could accept. Several times a week we paddled into Nanaimo to
collect our parcels. Clothes arrived, a tent, flashlights, energy
bars, contact lens solution, sunblock, life jackets, pocket knives,
flares, and much more. With a strange sense of the past echoing

through the present, I watched a heap of donated gear grow on our living-room floor.

The most important piece of our equipment was, of course, a kayak. We decided on a Feathercraft K2, a sophisticated boat with an aluminum frame and a nylon and synthetic rubber hull, which folds up into a bag measuring four feet by two. The Feathercraft company operates from Granville Island, a trendy section of Vancouver's waterfront. We rang the owners, Doug and Larry, and arranged to meet them to discuss the possibility of sponsorship.

Although we both hated dressing like hardy outdoors types, commuting by kayak had forced us into it. So a trip to Vancouver always gave us the chance to happily swap our practical waterproof jackets and fiber-pile sweaters for some fashionable city clothes, and we turned up at the Feathercraft workshop looking the antithesis of a couple about to embark on a year-long kayaking expedition. Doug and Larry, who were wearing fiber-pile sweaters, regarded us with mild suspicion. I handed them copies of our new expedition proposal (honed down, rewritten and excluding the "ideal couple" photos), my book and an article of mine just printed in the *Guardian*. They both skimmed through the newspaper article.

"You can obviously write . . . " said Doug.

His voice trailed off. As he stood there, lost for words, I saw us through his eyes: a couple of neophytes wearing clothes that would curl up at the sight of salt water.

I finished his thought for him. ". . . but you're wondering if we can kayak."

Our K2 Feathercraft was delivered to Protection Island a month before we were due to leave. While being filmed for a local television station, we assembled it for the first time. Back in their workshop, Doug and Larry had made it look easy. Now, I frantically paged through the instruction manual while Dag wrestled with aluminum tubing and plastic crossribs. Finally, we stood back and admired the finished product: a nineteen-foot-long bright red, brand-new kayak. The cameraman patted its hull.

"You're going a long way, baby," he told it. Then he turned to us. "When are you flying out?"

"We're not sure of the exact date," I said. "We haven't booked our tickets yet."

The look on his face told us it was time we did.

We'd left this "minor" detail to the last minute, thinking it would be a simple, straightforward matter. It wasn't. The travel agents we spoke to were all terse, overworked and infuriated by us.

"Round the world," they'd begin. "No problem. Northern or southern hemisphere?"

"Both."

"Ah. More complicated. What are your proposed destinations?"

I'd begin to reel them off: the Solomon Islands, India . . .

"That's not just around the world," said one. "That's up, down and all over the place."

Put more precisely, our route was a gigantic W, which would take us and our boat into five continents and across the equator four times. Each of the travel agents claimed that working out a price for such a complicated itinerary took hours.

"I'll do it," said the most enterprising, "if you promise to buy the ticket from me."

"How can I promise if I don't know what it will cost?"

"That's your problem," she haughtily responded.

Impressed by such audacity, I told her to go ahead. Her price was the best, so we booked and paid for the tickets there and then, over the phone.

"Now this kayak you mentioned," she said. "How much does it weigh?"

Her simple question heralded one of those awful moments when you know that you're about to hear bad news.

"Because once you've flown out of North America," she continued, "your weight limit is usually around twenty kilograms per person, and the excess baggage charge is 1 percent of the first-class fare, per kilo, per flight."

It didn't take a mathematical genius to work out that this meant an awful lot of money.

"It's impossible! We'll be carrying a hundred and twenty kilos!" One of our cats fearfully peered from beneath the sofa as Dag paced our living-room floor, loudly ranting. "On every flight, the excess will cost us the same as the first-class fare! Do you know how much first-class fares are? We can't do it!"

Once again, I cast my mind back a decade. I remembered all the times I'd said good-bye to my mountaineering boyfriend at Heathrow Airport. He always seemed to be on good terms with some official who would smooth out any problems concerning the heaps of excess baggage. If he could do it, I thought, so can I. Picking up the phone, I began contacting the airlines.

If I could chose someone for beatification, it would be Bill Duplak, the Western Canada manager of Qantas. He thought our forthcoming trip was a splendid idea. He arranged for our luggage to be transported free of charge on all our Qantas flights. This would take us as far as Hong Kong, where we would transfer to British Airways.

"I don't mean to be unprofessional," advised Bill, "but the Brits might be a bit sticky."

The Brits, in a word, said no. In vain, I begged, pleaded and cajoled.

"You may wish," said one particularly snooty woman, her plummy English tones only slightly tinged with a Toronto accent, "to negotiate this matter with airport managers en route. But I can't imagine you'll have much success."

With only weeks to go, our "to do" lists were reaching mammoth proportions. We sent off parcels around the world: supplies of contact lens solutions, suntan cream, mosquito repellent, spare parts for the boat, and clothes and a sleeping bag for the colder areas. We made a will and took out life insurance. We found tenants for our house and started packing away our belongings. Dag, who trained as a vet, put together a large, comprehensive medical kit. At a tropical health clinic, we loaded up on antimalaria pills and were given a battery of injections by a nurse who insisted we didn't need to be inoculated against cholera.

"But we're going to kayak down the Ganges," I told her.

"In that case you'll definitely need cholera injections!" she cried.

Friends constantly invited us for dinner, and one honest soul admitted, "I felt I had to cook for you, because I might never see you again."

She wasn't the only one who was worried. Despite all the furious preplanning, at this point neither of us could see beyond flying to the Solomon Islands, assembling the kayak and paddling off—into what? The bald truth was that we were heading for the tropics, of which we had no previous experience, and to a country about which we'd been able to glean precious little information. Even people who had worked in the South Pacific—and this also went for our destinations in India and Africa—were of little help. Because of our mode of travel, they said, we would be reaching areas that few outsiders ever got to. They could advise us on cultural mores and on what medicines to take, but they couldn't tell us what to expect.

Finally, eighteen months after that taxi ride in Mexico, we were as ready as we'd ever be to set off around the world with our kayak. It was the perfect excuse for a party.

Our friends presented us with a book entitled *Shark Attack* and a card depicting two corpulent crocodiles lying on a beach surrounded by remnants of a canoe, paddles and life jackets. As the evening wore on we were nudged and winked at about the stunning sex life we'd enjoy on those balmy tropical nights, and advice was offered on what to do if we were disturbed in the act by a croc.

"Run around in circles!"

"Poke it in the eyes!"

"Don't even consider climbing a tree," said one friend cheerfully. "Crocs can stand on their tails, you know."

Of course, everyone wanted to see the boat. We assembled it watched by a crowd of people, little knowing that this was something to which we would soon become very accustomed. And then various friends asked to be taken out for a spin. Eventually, we laid the kayak on the deck of the house, and the party simply raged on around it. The last guests left around 4 A.M. I promptly went to bed, but Dag said he wanted to stay up to watch the dawn. At eight o'clock I woke with a start, realizing he wasn't in bed with me. It didn't take me long to find him. He was outside, fast asleep in the back cockpit of our brand-new kayak, with a blissful expression on his face and the sea breeze ruffling his hair.

It seemed like the best of omens.

2

Unexpected Luxury

The air smelled of sandalwood and exhaust fumes, and the piercing screeches and whistles of birds vied with the revving of jet engines. Porters with yellow flowers tucked behind their ears wheeled handcarts heaped with luggage across the tarmac toward Nandi Airport's tiny terminal.

"Welcome to Fiji! Nice rooms in Nandi Motel! Very cheap! I take you there!"

A squat man with a shock of frizzy hair tugged at my sleeve.

"Best taxi price! No tip!"

Fiji was as close to the Solomon Islands as our round-the-world air tickets could get us. From here we had to buy our own connecting flights, which left from Suva, half a day's drive from Nandi.

"How much to Suva?" I asked the taxi driver.

"Cheap! Best price, no tip! I help you with your baggage! Where is your baggage?"

I pointed over to where Dag was standing next to our two large red sacks. The driver picked up the end of the one containing the kayak, which weighed over 100 pounds, and promptly dropped it again.

"What's inside?" he demanded.

"A boat," Dag told him.

"Boats cost extra."

"How much?"

"Ten dollars," said the driver.

"Too much," said Dag.

"How much you say?" asked the driver.

"Five dollars."

"Hah!" snorted the driver. "You think I am a crazy man!"

Dag relishes the cut and thrust of bargaining, but it always make me feel like a heartless profiteer. The driver obviously sensed this.

"Madam," he pleaded, "I have a wife and five children! They must eat!"

"I'm terribly sorry," I said.

He kicked one of the bags. "These are so heavy, they ruin my car. I take these, then I need new tires, new suspension, new everything."

"I'll meet you halfway," said Dag. "Seven dollars, or I'll find another taxi."

"You try find one, you go!"

"Look after the bags, Maria," said Dag, and he strode off toward a group of parked taxis.

"Come back!" the driver cried, and set off in pursuit of him. I gazed at the bulging sacks and glumly wondered why we'd ever imagined we could drag this lot around the world. Suddenly, amid much handshaking and guffawing, Dag and the driver were back. Within minutes, the taxi was stuffed with our baggage and we were on our way to Suva.

We drove across the island of Vita Levu, through a landscape of sun-browned hills and lush sugar cane fields. Lines of washing hung outside shacks built of branches and corrugated iron. Men walked under the shade of brightly striped umbrellas, women carried bundles of firewood on their heads. We stopped at a roadside stall and bought green coconuts from a barefoot boy. With a huge machete, he chopped off the tops so we could drink the sweet, refreshing milk, then fashioned little spoons from the shell for us to scoop out the gelatinous flesh.

"I could live on this," I enthused.

"You'll probably have to," said Dag.

It took us over an hour to walk the mile from Suva's South Seas Hotel to the airline office in the center of town. This was our first time in the tropics, and we were like a pair of three-year-olds, wide-eyed with wonder and stopping every few minutes to minutely examine new discoveries: huge purple banana pods drooping on fruit-laden stalks, trees heavy with papayas, streets littered with frangipani and hibiscus blossoms. The soil was dark red and moist, the air rich with strange scents, the vegetation lush, voluptuous and blatantly fertile. Little wonder, we decided, that the tropics have a sexy image—although we were soon to be dissuaded from any carnal pleasure by the heat and humidity of our cell-like hotel room, which we shared with a resident family of shiny brown cockroaches.

We did however, manage to eat, and had a late lunch at Jake Tulele's Drop-in Lovo Caravan. Jake had nut-brown skin, broad bare feet and a cultured British accent. Although born and raised in Fiji, he had lived in England for fourteen years, served in the Royal Air Force and studied at the Southwest London School of Business. His converted caravan was garishly painted with pictures of taro leaves, parachutes and nautilus shells, and emblazoned with slogans such as "We serve with speed for your delicate taste. To the caravan with haste!" The fried fish he served us was delicious, but the baked taro root was as cloying and unpalatable as wallpaper paste.

"I can't eat this," I whispered to Dag, slipping the taro to the skinny cats that skulked around our feet.

"You'll probably have to live off it," he teased.

We told Jake of our plans to kayak in the Solomon Islands.

"What a super adventure," he said. "I hear it's a trifle backward, though. Hardly anyone ever goes there."

His sentiment was echoed by the airline official we met later that day.

"Few tourists go to Solomon Islands," she told us, "which is why the flights are so expensive."

The price she quoted made us gulp; it was way above our budget. Despondently, we returned to the South Seas Hotel. Lounging in rattan chairs on its veranda were two young Englishmen. One sported ripped shorts and blond dreadlocks, the other had a shaved head and a ring through his nose.

"I tried to get to the Solomons last week," commiserated the one with the nose ring. "I applied for a job crewing on a yacht, but the rich bastards who owned it wouldn't take me on."

Dag and I exchanged a glance. "Where was this yacht?" we asked him.

"Lautoka Marina, close to Nandi," he said, wiping his nose with the back of his hand. "It's probably still there. They seemed pretty choosy about who they'd take on board."

Twenty-four hours later we were in Lautoka, a rather grim sugar mill town, and on our way to the marina. Before we got there, however, a tropical rainstorm struck, and within minutes the main street was awash with mud and hopping with frogs. Not wanting to turn up at the marina looking like a pair of drowned rats, we scurried for shelter.

"Come and have some tea!" called a woman from a doorway. She was resplendent in a scarlet silk sari, and her gray hair was pulled tightly back into a bun. Above her, a sign was suspended from a bamboo pole. In childlike red lettering it announced:

S. S. MUDALIER'S
WESTERN COFFIN DEALER AND REFRESHMENT BAR

We stepped into a narrow, gloomy room with red brick walls and a creaking ceiling fan. A table and three chairs were arranged next to the door. At the back of the room, on rough wooden frames, several coffins were stacked up. Painted a matte black, with dull metal handles, they looked light and insubstantial, like stage props.

"Welcome!" cried Mrs. Mudalier, her smile flashing with gold. "I make you hot tea with bread and butter, very nice!"

While she fired up a kerosene stove, she told us she'd been born in Fiji, a descendent of indentured laborers brought from India to work in the sugar cane fields. The coffin business had been in her husband's family for years, and she'd recently branched out into refreshments.

"Do you sell many coffins?" I asked.

"Yes! Yes! People are always dying and it is good for us!"

She handed us cups of sweet, milky tea and a plate of buttered white buns. While we ate, she paced up and down, fiddling with her sari and plying us with questions. Where were we from? What were our professions? Why were we in Lautoka?

"We're on our way to the marina," Dag told her. "We're trying to get a ride to the Solomon Islands."

I could tell she wasn't listening. "Do you have any unmarried brothers?" she asked.

"Dag has one," I replied.

"Very hard to find a good husband for my daughter," she confided. "She is twenty-six and very short. But she is a good girl. Is your brother tall? What is his profession?"

"He builds pianos," Dag answered, mischievously adding, "but I'm sure he could turn his hand to coffins."

"Very good! Very good! My husband is getting old, he needs help! Do you have a photograph of your brother?"

Realizing how serious she was, I began casting about for a tactful excuse. "He has a girlfriend . . ." I began.

"I know, I know," said Mrs. Mudalier sadly. "In Canada all nice tall boys have girls already. They are not interested in my poor short daughter. You like more tea?"

After our fifth round of tea, the rain eased off and we continued on our way to the marina. About thirty yachts were anchored there. A tall blond man was scanning the billboard, and when we stuck up our notice, "Two cooks and their kayak seek passage to the Solomons," he read it, looked carefully at us, but said nothing.

"So what do we do?" I asked Dag.

"Come back tomorrow, I suppose," he answered.

The blond man cleared his throat. "I'm Soren, skipper of *Swedish Caprice*," he said, holding out his hand. "We're going to the Solomons and our cook is on holiday. Can you come aboard now for an interview?"

Early next morning, the red bag containing our folded boat disappeared into one of the *Swedish Caprice*'s voluminous holds. As Soren steered us out of Lautoka Harbour, Ole and Gael, the other crewmembers, showed us around our new home.

It was eighty feet long and had teak decks, an interior lined with highly polished mahogany, a computerized navigational system, electronically controlled sails, a fax machine, a dive compressor, a water desalinator, two fridges, two freezers, a washing machine and dryer, a VCR and a compact disc player with speakers all over the boat.

"It belongs to a Swedish businessman," explained Gael. "We're sailing it around the world for him. He only comes aboard once every few months."

She opened a door onto a cabin with a double bunk. "You'll sleep here."

"Ooh, look, it's got an en-suite bathroom," I enthused, gazing at the marble washstand and its bright brass taps.

"It's called a head, Maria," said Dag from the side of his mouth.

Ole smiled at me. "I take it you haven't sailed much."

"Only in a kayak," I admitted.

"You'll find this much easier," he said.

Up on deck, another surprise awaited us. We were cruising past tiny islets covered with palm trees and ringed with dazzling white sand. Where the encircling reefs appeared, the water changed from aquamarine to a translucent, glacial green, and appeared to be lit from beneath. Our mouths fell open at the scene.

"It's astonishing!" I cried.

"What is?" asked Soren.

"This," I said, waving my hands to encompass the panoramic view. "It's exactly how the South Seas are supposed to look . . . "

"It's a cliché!" Dag chipped in.

". . . just like a tourist poster!"

Thoughtfully, Soren scratched his head. "I've been here too long," he said. "It all looks normal to me."

Soon there was no land in sight and nothing to see except an occasional school of flying fish. The trade winds filled the sails and pushed us along at a steady twelve knots. Soren, Ole and Gael took turns on watch, and Dag and I prepared three meals a day. We adopted our usual cooking roles: I did the peeling, chopping and washing up, and he took over the creative work. A superb chef, he's able to whip up delicious meals from basic ingredients in adverse conditions, a skill honed by many kayak trips. On Swedish Caprice, he had a wealth of food to choose from—the freezers were stuffed with meats, fish and vegetables, the cupboard with dry and tinned foods, the fridge with fine French wines.

"Let's stick to something simple," he said when it was time for us to prepare the first night's dinner. Coq au vin may be simple to prepare in a kitchen on land, but in the galley of a yacht under sail it's quite another matter. Neither of us had yet developed the "lean," a technique for staying upright when the ship is keeling over, so we staggered about, Dag trying to dismember the chicken and me attempting to slice onions. The Pacific pressed and swirled at the porthole above the stove, and soon we both began to feel a little nauseous.

"How are things going?" asked Soren as he walked past the galley, perfectly balanced.

"Fine, fine!" we chorused.

Seconds later, hit by a rogue wave, *Swedish Caprice* pitched wildly. The chicken pieces took flight, the cupboard door I'd forgotten to clip shut spewed out spice jars, sauce bottles and a bag of flour which hit Dag squarely in the back and burst open, and I was catapulted into the arms of Soren, who narrowly missed being stabbed in the neck with the sharp vegetable knife I was still clutching.

Miraculously, however, the crew seemed happy with our food and our company. Soren even intimated that as extra deckhands were always welcome, maybe we should consider staying on the boat beyond the Solomons and up to the Philippines, where the owner was due to join it. The offer was tempting, especially during the balmy evenings on deck when we sat sipping wine and listening to the creaking of the rigging, the soothing rush of water against the hull, and the stories of our fellow crewmembers.

They had all stumbled by accident into this lifestyle. Gael had been invited by a friend to help deliver a newly built boat to its final destination.

"We spent five months sailing it from France to Mauritius," she said. "As soon as I got there, I was offered another crewing job. It took me two years to get back to France." This was her second jaunt at sea. Again, she'd been away from home for two years. "This time I don't know when I'll return," she said.

Soren had trained as an architect in Sweden, and before settling down to his career he decided to do a spot of sailing. He crewed on an Atlantic crossing, and ten years later had still not got around to designing houses. And Ole was supposed to be taking over his father's car business in Denmark, "but I keep putting it off—I can't imagine going from this to selling cars."

And we couldn't imagine leaving such luxury for months of rough traveling. But the folded kayak in the hold of *Swedish Caprice* kept tapping at our consciences. We pulled it out; we assembled it and lashed it to the railings on deck. I took to leaning against it while I was making notes; I fancied I could sense its disappointment in me.

After five days at sea we reached the island of Efate, in Vanuatu. Port Vila's marina was bristling with yacht masts flying Australian, New Zealand, British, French and American flags. And its thatched, open-walled clubhouse was packed with the yachts' owners—or "yachties" as they called themselves. They emanated a carefree sense of well-being that bordered on smugness. They all seemed to know each other, and there was a lot of loud greeting and back-slapping going on. And as it was "Happy Hour," they were drinking with a vengeance. Within minutes of a local band starting to belt out Western pop songs, the small dance floor was heaving, and Ole dragged me into its midst.

"Have you tried *kava*?" he yelled as we hopped about in time to the music.

"Once, in Fiji," I yelled back. "It didn't have much effect."

Kava is a mildly narcotic drink made from the roots of pepper shrubs. "The stuff here is the strongest in the South Pacific," he told me. "They get virgin boys to chew the roots!"

One of the yachties had joined the band on the stage. "I wanna sing 'Rawhide'!" he bawled into the microphone.

The crowd whistled its approval.

"Bring me a whip!" he commanded. "And buzzards!"

It seemed a good time to go and find some kava.

A taxi took Dag, Ole and me out of Port Vila and past fields of sugarcane and bananas. After a fifteen-minute drive we turned onto a dirt track and parked by a shed with a corrugated iron roof. Inside, a man stood behind a table set with a large kettle, a pile of half coconut shells and a cash box. A couple of hurricane lamps hung from the ceiling, but the few customers were slumped on benches in dark corners.

"Kava makes you sensitive to light and noise," whispered Ole.

One of the customers lurched over to the table, gulped down a half shell of kava, then staggered back to his corner. There was no conversation, only the wet sounds of hawking and spitting. No one seemed to have noticed our presence. I sat on a bench while Dag and Ole went up to the table. In the dim light, beneath the low roof and next to the small ni-Vanuatu who served them, they looked ridiculously tall, like elongated shadows. They returned with three brimming coconut shells. I looked suspiciously at mine, and took a hesitant sip. It was thick with sediment and, unlike the refreshing Fijian kava, it had an unpleasantly sour taste.

"What about hepatitis?" I whispered to Dag.

"You don't really think they've got virgins chewing roots in the back room, do you?" he replied, but I noticed that he hesitated before swallowing his portion. Before long, my lips and the inside of my mouth began to feel numb. Then my eyelids and legs became heavy. I decided against a refill, but my companions were soon onto their third round. When Ole went up for a fourth, he staggered slightly and had to lean on the table while the barman poured the kava. Beside me, Dag had begun to hawk and spit, and he was slouched over, resting his elbows on his knees. "I think we should go," I whispered to him.

"This stuff's great," he mumbled back.

Thankfully, the barman waved the kettle about to show it was empty, and I led the shuffling men to the waiting taxi.

Back at the bar things were winding up. The band had left, and the "Rawhide" man was playing a mouth organ for the few couples still jigging around the dance floor. The rest of our crew was nowhere in sight. To get from the dock to *Swedish Caprice* we had to walk along a length of planking ten feet above the water. Crossing it during the day was bad enough, but at night, under the influence of alcohol and kava, it was nerve-racking. Despite a few wobbly moments, we all made it. Someone else hadn't. Below decks all the lights were on and the stereo was playing full blast. A trail of puddles and wet footprints led to the door of our cabin. Inside, soaking wet clothes lay in a heap on the floor, and two crewmembers from another boat were curled up together on our bunk. Gael was nowhere to be found, and Soren's cabin door was firmly shut. Dag and Ole promptly passed out on sofas in the saloon and lay snoring with their mouths wide open.

I got a bottle of wine from the fridge, poured myself a drink, and went up on deck. Just beyond the marina grounds there was an open-air market. People came from surrounding islands to sell produce there; those who couldn't afford to rent a room for the night slept on sacks next to their bundles of fruit and vegetables. From where I sat I could see a couple of women wearing cotton dresses, lying side by side on the ground, their arms over their eyes to block out the glare from street lamps. A cat rubbed itself against their bare feet and ignored the long-tailed rats scuttling about. For awhile I pondered the incongruity of it all: returning from a sleazy bar to a yacht worth several million pounds, where I could sit, drink French wine and look at women too poor to afford a roof over their heads. A sense of unease settled over me. I went below, found an empty bunk and escaped into sleep.

The next day began slowly on *Swedish Caprice*, with people who didn't belong on board leaving and those who did returning. We ate a late breakfast on deck, bantering with the people on the boats moored either side of us. One was owned by a Californian who had made his fortune in stocks and bonds, the other by an Australian couple who had saved for ten years to buy a yacht and sail it around the world. They advised us on the best shops in town to buy imported foods, and they grumbled that there were no well-stocked, air-conditioned supermarkets like those in Lautoka or Honiara. Meanwhile, at the open-air market, women padded along on broad, bare feet, balancing baskets of pineapples and papayas on their heads, or sat on the hard baked mud with piles of taro neatly arranged on huge banana leaves. Chickens languished inside bamboo cages next to stalls selling tourist souvenirs—light cotton wraps called *sulus* and carvings and "grass" skirts made of recycled plastic.

"That's a swell kayak you have there," the Californian called over to me as I cleared away the dishes. "How many miles have you put on her?"

"About five," I told him. He thought I was joking.

From Port Vila we sailed to Espirito Santo, the biggest island in Vanuatu, and moored in a bay wrapped around with dense jungle. It was an ominous, brooding place, and oppressively hot. The sky was heavy with cumulus clouds, and during periodic showers, fat raindrops bounced off a flat, gray, silky sea. For the first time in years, Dag was ill. He had developed a nasty chest cold, and he lay sniveling and wheezing in our cabin while the rest of us dined on deck. As we were finishing dessert, two men came alongside in a dugout. Both wore only ragged shorts. Lying at their feet were a few parrot fish. We called out greetings but they simply stared up at us, their blank expressions giving no clue to their thoughts. Watching them paddle away, my feelings of unease crystallized into a realization. I wanted to be camping on beaches and cooking over a fire instead of sleeping between linen sheets and eating off china plates. I felt that *Swedish Caprice,* because of its size, its luxury and the wealth it represented, was putting an impenetrable barrier between me and the country I was traveling through. In bed, I shared these feelings with Dag.

"Our fancy kayak will seem just as alien to local people," he said.

"Yes, but I won't feel so bad," I feebly replied.

Illness had sapped Dag of his usual optimism. "It's not going to be easy. We'll be exposed to the elements and totally reliant on peoples' good nature. You might end up wishing you were back on *Swedish Caprice.*"

That night, I dreamed we were paddling our kayak through waters infested with sharks and crocodiles, that we both had malaria and that insects were crawling all over my body. Just before dawn, I awoke with the unmistakable signs of a bladder infection. Beside me, Dag was sweating with a fever.

During the five-day crossing to the Solomons, Dag's temperature steadily rose, and as well as a bladder infection I got motion sickness. Gael took over in the kitchen while I alternated between resolutely staring at the horizon from the deck and dashing to the toilet. By the third day at sea, unable to keep down any antibiotics, I had started to pass blood in my urine. Dag was becoming increasingly feverish and had a racking cough. On the morning of the fourth day, we looked out of our cabin porthole to see the southernmost tip of the Solomon Islands slipping by. For months we had stared at maps of this 900-mile-long archipelago and tried to imagine how it looked. At first sight, it was even more exotic than we'd expected. Lush jungle cloaked steep mountain ridges, clouds of mist hung in the valleys, and along the yellow beaches leaf houses stood on stilts over the water. A pod of pilot dolphins surfaced, and birdwing butterflies as big as our hands flapped by. We stared out of the porthole for almost an hour, then lay back, ruefully smiling at the irony of the situation. Here we were, at the first destination of our great adventure, and barely able to climb down from our bunk.

26

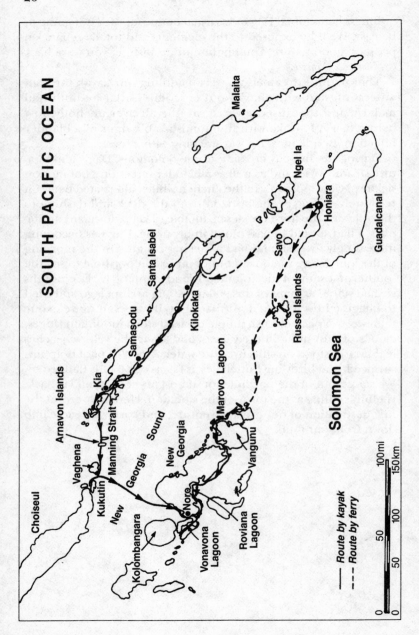

3

Hospital Horrors

"Your bodies are very hot," pronounced Dr. Pimbo Ogatuti. After feeling our foreheads and listening to our litany of symptoms, he disentangled a stethoscope from the three hanging around his neck and began to examine Dag's chest. "How much time will you spend in Honiara?" he asked us.

The answer to that, although we tried to say it tactfully, was as little as possible.

From what we'd seen so far of Honiara, the capital of the Solomon Islands, it wasn't a particularly appealing place. The main street was stiflingly hot and humid, and lined with dismal stores. Crowds of wild-looking young men hung about. They were small and muscular, with bare feet and bushy hair. Their cheeks bulged with betel nut, their lips and teeth were a nasty rust-brown color and the cracked pavement around them was splattered with their red saliva. They were some of Honiara's transient population, drawn to a city which had only one traffic light and one lift, but which was sophisticated beyond belief compared to their outlying villages. As we stumbled along past these men on our way to the doctor's office they gave us suspicious looks. This was hardly surprising: tourists were a fairly uncommon sight in Honiara, and we were a particularly sickly pair of specimens.

We told Dr. Ogatuti about our plans to spend three months kayaking in the Solomons, and that we needed to get well and fit again as soon as possible.

"Could we have some tests?" began Dag.

"Oh tests, silly tests! No need for those!" cried the doctor, scribbling out two prescriptions. "Soon you will be paddling your boat." Which was, of course, exactly what we wanted to hear.

Outside the Mendana Kitano Hotel, minibuses disgorged groups of elderly Japanese and American men, veterans of the Second World War who were revisiting the sites they once fought fierce battles over. In the open-walled lobby, lily-white Australian businessmen in shorts and long white socks sat drinking beer and reading week-old copies of the *Sydney Herald*. "It's expensive to stay here," one advised us. "But all the other places in town are shit pits."

A quick tour by taxi around Honiara's handful of hotels had revealed that his assessment was not far off the mark. Reassuring ourselves that it would only be for a few days, we checked into the Mendana Kitano. From the balcony of our room, we sadly waved good-bye to our friends on *Swedish Caprice* as they pulled up the anchor, motored out of Honiara harbor and headed north toward the Philippines.

"Listen to this," said Dag, reading from the local newspaper. "The Honiara Kilu'ufi Hospital authorities have confirmed that an amputated leg was found in a garden close to the hospital grounds. A principal nursing officer said that a dog must have stolen the leg from the incinerator before anyone had a chance to dispose of it."

We shuddered and laughed and said that we'd never put ourselves at the mercy of such a place. Two days later, with Dag's temperature at a steady 104 degrees and me with such pain in my kidneys that I could no longer stand up straight, we had no choice in the matter.

A morose receptionist sat behind a glass slatted window with names written into the thick dust. "You need Dr. O'Brien in the Guadalcanal Referral Clinic," she informed us. "Go through the emergency ward and around the corner."

The ward had about ten beds covered with rumpled gray sheets. A man was doubled in pain, three small children huddled together and several women lay with babies at their breasts. At a table, a teenager sat clutching his arm and groaning loudly. There wasn't a doctor or nurse in sight.

In blinding sunshine, we sat on a bench waiting our turn to see Dr. O'Brien. Next to us was a young mother and her two children. They had coarse, straw-blond hair and the scars of ritual cuts on their brown cheeks. All three of them gave us sympathetic looks.

"Youpelas sick?" asked the woman shyly.

"Yes," I told her. "Fever."

"Fevi?" she nodded wisely. "Youpelas plenti sick."

Dr. O'Brien was a brisk man from Northern Ireland. He prescribed a different drug for me and, brushing aside Dag's requests for sputum tests and an X-ray, sent him off to the laboratory for a blood test. As we climbed the stairs to the lab, a white-coated woman came past us carrying a cardboard box filled with blood samples. One of the vials had fallen over, and blood was running over her hands and dripping through the bottom of the box.

Dag was instructed to take his blood sample to the Malaria Lab. "Follow the arrows," he was told. The arrows led back down the blood-spotted stairs and along a grimy wall to a boarded-up window with a sign that said KNOCK AND WAIT.

We did. The board slid back, and from a dark interior a hand reached out and grabbed the vial from Dag.

"Fifteen minutes!" announced a disembodied voice.

Gingerly, we stepped across an open drain filled with purple water, slime and bits of cardboard, and entered the "waiting-room," which was a piece of corrugated iron balanced on concrete posts. Around it, tall irises were in full bloom, their yellow flowers shaking in the breeze.

"Mr. Goning!" A hand thrust a white piece of paper from the dark window.

"That must be you," I said.

Dag recrossed the drain and took the paper.

"The test was positive!" he said in dismay.

We scrutinized the result slip. Dat Goning, Canadian, Positive.

"Mr. Goning!"

This time, a head poked through the window. "Give me your result, please!"

The paper was snatched back inside, then thrust out again moments later. The "Positive" stamp had been scratched out and "Negative" handwritten beneath it.

"Mistake!" cried the disembodied voice.

"I'm sure it's nothing serious," said Dr. O'Brien. "The climate here always gets to tourists when they first arrive. Finish off the course of drugs that Dr. Ogatuti prescribed. That should sort you out."

On our way back to the Mendana Hotel, we stopped off at the shipping office and booked tickets for the following Sunday's sailing to New Georgia Province, where we planned to do the first part of our kayak trip. That gave us six days—ample time, we thought—to recuperate.

The week passed in a haze of pain and fever. We rarely left our hotel room. By day, we listened to the clinking and chattering from the open-air bar below us, and at night the tinny recorded music of the hotel's Gilbertese dance troupe pounded through our walls. When the maids came to clean the room, we sat on the balcony and looked longingly at the ocean. Gradually, my infection began to retreat, but Dag showed no sign of improvement. He had eaten little for two weeks, and he was exhausted by coughing and delirium. A day after our ship sailed, we were back at the hospital. After sitting in the sun outside the doctor's office, Dag passed out.

"Good God," said O'Brien. "How did he get into this state?"

An X-ray showed a shadow on Dag's lung. Pneumonia and pleurisy were diagnosed and a suitable drug prescribed. Within forty-eight hours his temperature was down, his appetite had began to return, and we'd rebooked our tickets to New Georgia Province.

It didn't take us long to provision for our trip, because there was little to choose from. From the Chinese-owned supermarkets we bought rice, tinned fish, sugar, milk powder, tea, and, after a long, hard search, some garlic. Honiara's market was a sad affair: beneath black umbrellas set up on sun-baked mud were pathetic little piles of peanuts, withered bundles of green onions and stalks of overripe bananas. To supplement the trade items we had brought from Canada—fishing lures and line, needles, thread, balloons—we purchased some of the tobacco that was coiled up like thick rope. Then we had lunch at one of the food stalls on the edge of the market. Posted next to the counter was a large, formidable notice:

TO ALL CUSTOMERS
– Do not sit down and tell stories
– Do not eat food from other snack bars here
– Do not move the chairs from one table to another
– Do not chew betel nut and spit around here
– If you have no business to conduct here
GET LOST!

Quickly, we ate our chicken and rice and left.

That night, we spread the parts of our kayak over the hotel patio to check that nothing had been damaged during the journey from Canada. One of the lily-white Australians wandered over to us, clutching his beer can inside a polystyrene holder.

"What's all this about?" he asked.

We told him of our plan to go to New Georgia Province and kayak through Marovo Lagoon, reputed to be the largest island-bound lagoon in the world, and on to the smaller Roviana and Vonavona Lagoons. And then, to travel to Isabel Province, where we would kayak the length of Santa Isabel Island and cross the Manning Strait to Vaghena Island.

"Christ, that sounds like a lot of bloody hard work," he commented. "Especially for a pair of saplings like you!"

"You can hardly blame him," said Dag later, as we were preparing for bed. "Just look at us!"

Side by side, we surveyed our reflections in the full-length mirror. After weeks of illness, Dag's once muscular legs now looked like they belonged to a chicken, while my skinny frame and scrawny neck made me resemble a praying mantis.

"Five years of kayaking," I said, quoting from our original sponsorship proposal, "have honed this couple's survival skills and developed their stamina!"

"Don't make me laugh!" Dag protested. "It hurts my chest!"

Stifling our mirth, we fell into bed. Ready or not, we were setting off in the morning.

4

Drawbacks of Paradise

The *Iuminau* sat by Honiara's wharf, puffing smoke from its funnels like a contented old man with a pipe. Three hours before it sailed, this rusty ferry boat seemed full to capacity. The toilets were already overflowing and the air-conditioned first-class lounge smelled of vomit. We heaved our baggage up a narrow stairway to the top deck, where there was what appeared to be a convention of representatives from every corner of Melanesia. Among the solid mass of people were skin colors ranging from pale brown to ebony, and hair from black and tightly frizzed to straw yellow and straight. Men reclined on mats, chewing sticks of sugar cane. Women leaned against sacks of betel and coconuts. Around them were heaped stalks of bananas, and live pigs lay trussed and wrapped in bright cloth. When we appeared there was a flurry of good-natured shuffling and rearranging. Hands reached up to help us with our baggage, and soon we were comfortably settled down. As yet more passengers came aboard, the good-natured shuffling continued, until I was practically sitting on top of a small child, who regarded me with an unblinking stare while her father picked through her hair for nits.

When the *Iuminau* was an hour out into New Georgia Sound, an elderly man clad only in shorts began weaving his way through the crowd toward where we sat.

"Where are your children?" asked Jim Kolikeda when he reached us.

On hearing we had none, his face fell.

"I am so sorry. I will pray that God sends you a son."

Jim was a retired schoolteacher from the village of Mbili, where, in thirteen hours' time, we were planning to disembark and begin our journey by kayak through Marovo Lagoon. He was also an active member of the Seventh Day Adventist Church, and as the only white people on deck he'd targeted us for a donation.

"Who has invited you to stay at Mbili?" he asked, as he wrote out a receipt for the money we'd given him.

We admitted to knowing no one there.

"The people believe the night is full of spirits," he said. "They will be afraid when they see two white people appear from the darkness. I will tell them that you are my *wantoks* from overseas, and that you have come to stay in my house."

Wantoks is a loose term referring to relatives and close friends. Custom demands that Solomon Islanders always help their wantoks, even if they turned up uninvited and unannounced. Jim assured us that his explanation of our sudden appearance would perfectly satisfy his neighbors.

We met the only other tourist on board when he emerged from the first-class lounge and came up on deck to get warm. He was a small, handsome Austrian with a walrus mustache, wearing the sort of clothes a mercenary might favor, with lots of pockets for bullets and guns. He told us that he worked as a receptionist at one of Salzburg's top hotels, and during his annual holiday he always headed off to some far-flung place. But the Solomons, it appeared, had been flung a bit too far for his taste.

"In first class, it is like the Arctic," he complained, "and one woman is vomiting. Out here," he swept his arm around to encompass sacks and baskets and grunting, wet-nosed pigs, "it is hell. If I brought my mother here from Vienna, she would have a heart attack and die."

When he had returned to first class, a man who had watched our exchange curiously leaned forward and asked if we lived in the same village as the man we'd been speaking to.

"Em wantok bilong yu?" he asked. "Is he your relation?"

No amount of explanation could persuade him that we'd never met the Austrian before.

Toward midnight the *Iuminau's* engines slowed and an anchor was dropped.

"Here is Mbili," said Jim.

Beyond the ferry there was only utter blackness, without even a twinkle of light to signal a village or a harbor. From the dark, two motorized dugouts materialized. We were instructed to get into one of them, and our baggage was perched precariously atop sacks and cloth-wrapped bundles in the other canoe, which slid away into the night.

Ten minutes later, our dugout ran onto a beach. Fireflies twinkled between trees, and the air was damp and sweetly scented. Our bags lay on the sand a few yards away; with impressive ease, Jim hoisted the one containing the kayak onto his shoulder and padded off along a path through the trees, while we struggled along behind him with the rest of our belongings. His house stood on stilts and had an iron roof, plywood walls and thatched window shutters propped open with twigs. From a back room came the snuffling and crying of children. Jim's wife, Linethy, greeted us. She was a rotund woman with a direct manner.

"You want the toilet?" she asked, and led me back along the path to a rocky section of beach, where she turned away to give me privacy.

That first night in Mbili, sleep was impossible. Our bed was a mat in a corner of the main room. Above us the tin roof seemed to steadily release all the heat it had stored up during the day. We lay as far away from each other as our sheet sleeping bag would allow, sweating profusely and panting like dogs on a summer's day. Mosquitoes whined around our ears. Cats fought beneath the house, and a neighbor's baby wailed unremittingly. While it was still dark, roosters began warming up their vocal cords. As light seeped through the windows, chickens squawked, dogs barked and someone revved up an outboard engine. Then one of Jim's children came out of her bedroom, took one look at us and burst into terrified screeching.

With Jim and Linethy we shared a breakfast of pawpaw, coconut biscuits we'd bought in Honiara and water from the rain catchment tank. As Mbili was a Seventh Day Adventist village, its inhabitants were forbidden tea, coffee or alcohol.

"Sometimes your wantoks come in their yachts," said Jim, "and they bring us many problems. They trade beer and whisky for carvings, they give our young men bad ideas. And then they go with spears onto our reefs and they catch our fish without permission, without compensation! You must tell your wantoks not to do such things!"

Almost every inch of land in the Solomons is privately owned under a complicated system of customary tenure. Primary landowners, like Jim, have the final say over what happens to the land, while secondary owners have the right to live and grow food on the land and fish off the surrounding reefs. As 90 percent of Solomon Islanders live from subsistence fishing and farming, these rights are jealously guarded and the subject of much legal wrangling. We got the impression that if we camped or fished without permission, it would be comparable to us discovering that a total stranger had spent the night in our spare bedroom and helped himself to the contents of our fridge. When we took out our map of Marovo Lagoon to show Jim our intended route, he swept a finger across its bottom end, encompassing islets, reefs and ocean.

"This is all my land," he told us, grinning broadly. "I give you permission to stay there. You have been very generous to our church, there will be no charge."

It took us an hour to put the kayak together, and almost as long to pack it. From beneath the shade of an enormous banyan tree, a crowd of villagers watched mesmerized as we fiddled about with waterproof bags and camera boxes, arguing over what should go where. Their curiosity turned to pure astonishment when we set about protecting ourselves from the sun. We donned sunglasses and canvas hats, and smeared every inch of exposed flesh with sunblock cream.

"They want to know why you are doing these strange things," said Jim.

We explained that without the glasses we would be blinded by the dazzling light, and without the hats and cream the sun would turn our skins the color of a red hibiscus blossom. The villagers gave us pitying looks, and we paddled away feeling rather foolish.

The lagoon stretched away before us for over sixty miles. It was sprinkled with jungle-clad islets, as if New Georgia Island had once shaken itself in a fit of fury and tossed fragments of its mountainous spine into the sea. Paddling toward their shores, we were met by wafts of warm, fragrant air, and sometimes a large fruit bat languorously flapped out from the trees to circle us, as if sent by some unseen but watchful presence deep in the forest.

This was the jungle of my childhood fantasies, inhabited by huge, strangely shaped trees draped with hanging vines, the day shut out by a dense canopy of leaves, the darkness pierced by shafts of light in which insects danced and weaved. There was no disputing the beauty of the place, but paradise has its drawbacks, especially when you're not acclimatized to it. The temperature was around 90 degrees, and humidity was almost 100 percent. Sweat streamed off my face, my sunglasses slid down my nose, my wide-brimmed hat became unbearably heavy and I was convinced I was paddling through treacle. After two hours we had covered only three miles, and we were exhausted. There were no beaches in sight, only islets ringed by mangrove swamps. In one of these swamps we found some shade beneath the spiky leaves of a gigantic succulent plant.

"Do you think I can get out to pee?" I asked Dag. "What about crocs?"

"Jim told me that crocodiles have been hunted to extinction in Marovo Lagoon," he said.

"How does Jim know?"

"Because he lives here."

"Marovo Lagoon's a big place."

"Local knowledge is always the most reliable source of information, Maria," said Dag archly.

Only partially reassured, I hopped out of the boat and balanced on a thick root.

Since leaving Mbili we'd not seen a soul, but as soon as I pulled down my shorts a man in a dugout suddenly appeared from the mangrove thickets. Luckily any prurient interest he may have had in a debagged white woman was diverted by the kayak. Like most Solomon Islanders, he'd learned how to paddle a dugout almost before he could walk, but this was the first time he'd seen a canoe such as ours. He leaned over it, stroked the hull, put his head right inside the front cockpit to examine the construction of this strange and wonderful boat. Dag explained how it could be folded up and stored in a bag.

"Really, you break it up?" he asked. "You put it in a basket?"

His name was Montgomery, and he was returning home to his village some miles away after working in his garden on this islet.

He showed us the way to Njapuana, one of the lagoon's boundary islands, which had the only sand beach for miles and where

Jim had given us permission to camp. From a distance it looked ideal, shaded by leaning coconut palms. As we glided toward shore, one of the coconuts plummeted down and splashed into the water. Another hurtled itself at us while we were dragging the kayak up the beach and made a sizable crater in the sand a few feet away. By the time we'd found a missile-free spot and established camp I was dribbling with sweat. Longingly, I gazed out at the lagoon.

"Mi suim long hia?" I asked Montgomery, who was now engrossed in a thorough examination of our tent. "Can I swim here?"

"Yesss," he replied.

Dag pointed beyond the turquoise shallows to the deeper emerald water where the coral reef ended in a steep drop-off.

"Gat bigfela sharks long hia?" he asked. "Are there sharks here?"

"Yesss."

"Oh well," said Dag. "There are sharks all over the Solomons. We can't spend the next few months worrying about them."

Donning our snorkels, we went in. Dag headed for the drop-off, but I decided to stay in the shallows. Minutes later, I saw a baby shark. It was about ten inches long, with a large head, a pudgy body and fat fins. It looked so like a stuffed toy that I gazed at it without fear. But then another shark, too big to be a toy, appeared. It was five feet long, with a sleek white body tipped with black. It came up from behind me and seemed to turn its head to look in my direction before it swam away. Splashing and spluttering, I headed for the beach and hit the sand on all fours.

Dag, who had heard the commotion I made, followed me in and stood waist-deep in water, sternly lecturing me. "That was only a harmless reef shark! But if you act like a wounded fish you'll attract every dangerous shark for miles around!"

Obviously, I already had, because minutes later it was his turn to scramble ashore. "I just came face to face with a hammerhead! At least twelve feet long! It swam right by me, just beyond the drop-off, it was moving like a train!"

"Bigfela shark," I told Montgomery. "Hammerhead."

He shrugged. "Hammerhead im no gat tis," he said nonchalantly.

"No teeth?" I repeated incredulously.

"Im tru," he insisted. "It's true."
My faith in local knowledge crumbled.

We were woken at dawn by something pattering on the dome roof of our tent. Scattered over the beach were fist-sized blossoms with pinky-white petals cradling long scarlet stamens. They were dropping from the trees above us, and on impact with our tent and the sand they released a sweet, heady scent. The lagoon was still as glass; a shimmering lizard darted over my feet; a white cockatoo with lemon tail-feathers flashed past; parrots chattered in the branches above my head. It was November, a month I usually spent wrapped in bulky sweaters and socks, yet here I was, before sun-up, clad only in a *sulu,* a light cotton wrap.

"This," I wrote in my notes, "feels like nothing short of a miracle." For several days we wandered amid the lagoon's myriad islets. The ocean was calm and lambent. The only sounds we heard were the natural ones of wind, water and birds, and the night skies were undimmed by any electric glow. Gradually, we established the rhythms and routines necessary for us to survive months sharing a small boat and a small tent. We divided up the work involved in packing and unpacking the kayak, in breaking and setting up camp. We created individual personal space: the left of the tent next to the sleeping mat was mine, the right was Dag's. Quickly, life was whittled down to a simple, satisfying core. We had one change of clothes each, and ate mostly fish, rice and coconuts. Our decisions concerned how many miles to cover each day and where to spend each night. Our worries were about finding drinking water and staying healthy. This last consideration, because of our isolation and vulnerability, was a fairly weighty one. We religiously took our malaria medication. To prevent small skin cuts or scrapes from festering we immediately treated them with tincture of iodine. Fungal infections flourished on us: Dag developed something he referred to as "crotch rot," I got vaginal thrush and we both had athlete's foot. Every night, smothered in various powders and creams and sprayed with a noxious mosquito repellent, we lay sweating in the tent, wondering what had happened to the stunning sex life our friends had forecast for us.

Those same friends had filled me with dread about sharks and crocodiles, but we quickly realized that we were in far more danger from the tiny malarial mosquito. One afternoon, after paddling past endless mangrove swamps and despairing of finding a campsite, we came across a clearing in the jungle a few feet from shore. Wild orchids grew waist-high around a patch of ground covered by dried palm leaves. Gratefully, we set up our tent, then went snorkeling over the reef. Rainbow-hued parrot fish munched noisily on purple coral heads as big as tabletops; a small iridescent squid moved in a pulsing rhythm. So engrossed were we by this marine world that we failed to realize what was happening above water. A cloud of mosquitoes had risen from our delightful orchid garden and was homing in on the two floating hunks of pink flesh. Too late, we made a dash for cover, hotly pursued by the cloud, some bits of which ended up zipped into the tent with us. After a frantic half-hour of exterminating the mosquitoes, we had no choice but to settle in for the night, even though it was barely past four o'clock and unmercifully hot. Trying not to scratch our bites, we watched and listened as the whining beasties outside worked themselves into a frenzy. They covered the tent, swarming over the insect screens and poking their proboscises through the tiny holes. Dag took my eyebrow tweezers and began exacting his revenge, but it was a fruitless task: there were thousands more for every mosquito he managed to put out of action. Dinner was a dispiriting affair: a tin of second-grade Solomon Blue tuna fish, which resembled cat food in texture and taste, and a packet of Hard Navy biscuits, which were stale and soggy. Then we lay, and sweated, and listened to the surrounding jungle. Something crashed through branches, piercing screams echoed around, water dripped from foliage, insects whirred, frogs croaked, and land crabs rustled across the dried palm leaves. Inadvertently, we'd pitched our tent over the hole of a crab, which spent much of the night tirelessly trying to scrabble its way though our groundsheet.

Sleeping in the leaf huts of villages was infinitely more pleasurable. In Chubikopi, on Vangunu Island, we were invited to stay with the family of David Livingstone Nonga. The houses of Chubikopi stood on stilts over the water. Behind them was a steep forested hillside with areas cleared for gardens. As we'd paddled toward the village, children ran along the shore, whooping in excitement, and adults gathered on verandas to watch our approach. Their shyness had been quickly overcome by curiosity.

"What happens to this boat in big seas?" the men asked as we tied it to one of the house stilts. "Why do the paddles have two blades? What is the purpose of this journey?"

While Dag talked to the men, the women beckoned me up to a veranda. Gratefully, I stepped into a cool, airy house. The floor was made of bamboo and mangrove wood slats, the walls and roof of dried pandanus leaves, and everything was sewed or tied with vine. I removed my sunglasses and hat, and my hair fell around my face in lank, sweat-soaked strands. The women giggled and whispered to each other in a soft language that sounded like Italian. Children peered at me from behind the safety of their mothers; one reached out and tentatively touched the hairs on my arm, another stared suspiciously at my sandals.

David took us on a tour of the village, along a path made of coconut husks. Around each house, the dirt had been meticulously swept, and there were flower beds full of exotic irises. We stopped briefly at the village store. It was an ugly structure of wood and iron, inside as hot as an oven and with little for sale, but David was inordinately proud of it. "It is a permanent building," he boasted. "Everyone in the village wants a house like this, with an iron roof and a rain tank to collect water, but few can afford it."

The other permanent building in Chubikopi was the elementary school. It had two rooms and crushed coral floors. There were no desks or benches, no furniture of any kind except a couple of ancient blackboards. One hundred and twenty pupils studied there, and only a fraction of these would go on to one of the country's handful of secondary schools. "When a pupil wins a scholarship to secondary school," David told us, "everyone in the village helps his family to buy his clothes and books."

In a smoky cooking hut I helped David's wife Merver prepare dinner. While she wrapped taro and cassava roots in banana leaves and laid them on hot stones, I worked on the slippery cabbage, discarding each stem and shredding the leaves. Outside the hut, her eldest son sat astride a log, vigorously grating the innards of coconut shells. He heaped the flesh into a bowl and squeezed out its thick, white juice. Merver stirred this into some warm water, added the cabbage and the contents of a tin of tuna we'd brought, and let the lot simmer gently over the fire.

"When I saw you in your canoe I wanted to laugh," she said. "White people paddling! It is our custom to paddle, not yours!"

She was surprised to learn that Dag and I were married. "I heard that white people do not do this. How much did he pay for you?"

"Nothing," I told her.

"Nothing!" Her eyes widened. "No bride price? For me, David had to give many pigs, yams and mats!"

I asked how she had met David.

"My parents told me I had to marry him. They said he was a good man and would look after me."

"Were you happy?"

"I was very cross!"

"Could you have refused to marry him?"

"No. Too much trouble."

"Were your parents right? Is he a good man?"

"He is not lazy. Some people here have not one cent to buy kerosene or soap, but they can grow food to eat and cut down sago palm to make their house. But some people are too lazy to make a garden or a house, so they go to their wantoks and depend on them."

All afternoon, two of David's wantoks had been lying on the veranda, chewing betel and resting their heads on empty Coca-Cola tins. When we carried the food to the house they were still there, and they sat up to eat. Everything had a strong smoky taste, and I found the taro cloying and difficult to swallow. Merver was closely watching me, and she hurried off to fetch a jug of water and two brand-new glasses that still had labels stuck to them. "We hear that foreigners drink water with their food," she said.

After a brief, spectacular sunset, darkness fell like a curtain. Beyond the veranda, frogs croaked and fruit bats squabbled in the trees. Huge bugs dived at the kerosene lamp, and four children lay around it on their stomachs, paging through a twenty-year-old copy of *National Geographic*. When I asked Merver the ages of her children, she looked vague.

"This one was born in the season of the ngali nut," she said, pointing to the biggest. "And that one in the season of the pineapple."

We slept out on the veranda. Toward dawn, I was woken by an archer fish which missed its insect prey and squirted me through the split bamboo floor. For a few minutes I lay listening to the slap of the ocean against the stilts of the house, the regular breathing of the family in the rooms inside, a gecko rustling in the leaf thatch above my head, the pops and trills of birds in the jungle. Opening my eyes, I peered down through the floor slats: our kayak bobbed peacefully about next to David's dugout canoe. The sky was streaked with pink and violet, and there was an orange glow on the horizon. I crept down the steps of the veranda and over to the outhouse. It was also built of thatch, and stood on stilts over the water. In the pig pen standing next to it, a large sow snuffled and snorted at me through the bars.

When I returned to the veranda, David was up.

"Will you drink tea with us?" he asked.

He was horrified to learn that I had presumed Chubikopi to be a Seventh Day Adventist Village.

"We are in the United Missionary Church! The SDAs are bad people, they come from America with much money, they preach damnation, they forbid people to dance, they steal our congregations. When you were at Mbili, I hope you did not give money to the SDA church!"

Before leaving Chubikopi, we gave David some fishing hooks and line, balloons for his children and a donation for the school. In the Solomons, receiving a gift is akin to going into debt, as whatever is accepted must in due course be paid back, and David looked nervous as he accepted our offerings. "Repayment for your hospitality," we assured him.

"It is too much," he said. "Now we must feel obliged to give you something more."

We paddled away with his gift of cassava and coconut strapped on to the deck of the kayak.

5

Hunted Heads

"Will there be another war?" cried Chief Nathan, peering at us through grease-smeared spectacles.

After ten days in Marovo Lagoon, we'd surfed across its outer reef at a spot called Hele Bar, then headed along the exposed southwest coast of New Georgia Island. It was late afternoon by the time we slipped between two offshore islands and into the shelter of Roviana Lagoon. About a mile along it we came across a permanent house on stilts close to the water, and Chief Nathan had anxiously hurried out and beckoned us ashore.

"In 1941," he told us, "a Japanese man came here in a boat like yours. One year later, the Second World War began. I remember watching the tops of palm trees being shot off. There was such noise, such suffering. The war ended, the trees grew over the crashed planes, once more we had peace and quiet. Today, when I looked through my window and saw you in your boat, I was much afraid. I said to my wife that another war is coming to Roviana Lagoon."

A rainstorm had followed us across the lagoon, and Nathan hurried us inside his house. He told us he was eighty-two years old, the custom owner of five villages, and was in the midst of a legal wrangle over land rights. He seemed to positively relish the thought of going to court.

"I will win!" he said gleefully. "I always win because for years I have written down every fact of my life!"

Before we left, he took out a grease-stained exercise book

and wrote down our names, ages, the fact that we had no children and our assurances that we were not another harbinger of war.

As we paddled to an islet owned by Chief Nathan, we met a man fishing from a dugout canoe. He was using a twig, a piece of string and a scrap of cloth for bait.

"Yu laikim yangfela coconuts?" he asked, and passed us two green coconuts from the bottom of his boat.

We drank the juice and ate the flesh of the coconuts as an appetizer to our dinner of boiled rice and fried green onions. We'd traded for the onions in Marovo Lagoon the previous day, and now they were crawling with large ants which we carefully blew out of the stalks before chopping the onions up. The man reappeared, and proudly presented us with a small parrot fish.

"I bet it's his only catch of the day," said Dag, but we couldn't refuse. In thanks, we gave him some nylon fishing line and a brightly colored lure. At first he was speechless, then he insisted he was going to paddle five miles to his village and back again to bring us potatoes. We managed to persuade him to stay with us and share our meal instead. While the fish cooked, I asked him if there were any crocodiles in Roviana Lagoon.

"Plenti pukpuk!" he replied. "Tumora, you twofelas kam long ples bilong me, and lukluk long pukpuk."

"He wants us to visit his village tomorrow and see the crocodiles," said Dag, interpreting my blank look as incomprehension of the man's pidgin. In fact I had understood, but wished I hadn't.

A baby saltwater crocodile lay panting in the bottom of a Second World War petrol tank. Adolescent crocs stared at us from inside bamboo cages with banana leaf roofs. The grownups, a male and a female, were in separate enclosures made of split logs driven into the ground and lashed together with vine. I peered over the logs at the female. She appeared to be sleeping in the sun, her mouth wide open.

"Don't get too close!" cried Likey, the English-speaking son of the man who had invited us to Nusa Hope.

The crocodile's legs seemed to suddenly grow and lengthen beneath her, and with her jaws snapping she made a furious dash at me across the enclosure and threw herself against the logs. They quivered, and held.

"She thinks you want her eggs," Likey explained, referring to the contents of the large mound of earth in the middle of the enclosure.

"Tell her I don't," I said, rapidly retreating from the rather insubstantial barrier that separated me from six feet of deadly reptile. "Most definitely not."

Silas, the old man who kept the crocodiles as mascots, came out to meet us. He was adorned with a shell necklace and a wreath of frangipani blossom. His wife hovered in the shadows of their hut, trying to get a peek of me while I tried to get a peek of her. Her bare chest was intricately tattooed, and her long earlobes sported huge holes, stretched by years of wearing heavy clamshell earrings. Silas talked nonstop in Roviana, a dialect of which we understood not one word.

"He says he feeds the crocodiles on chickens, pigs and dogs," Likey told us.

"Live ones?" I asked.

"They are live until he puts them in the pen. Then they die of fright."

Our appearance in the village had emptied the school of its pupils. A teacher was running around with a bamboo stick, vainly trying to round up his flock and herd it back to the classrooms. Finally, he started furiously ringing the bell. This had an instantaneous effect on the children, who took to their heels and raced away amid a cloud of dust.

"Where do the crocodiles come from?" I asked Likey.

He stared at me as if I'd gone mad.

"From here," he replied, waving his arms around to indicate the lagoon and its mangrove-lined shores.

After a last, rather nervous look at the crocodiles, we carried on with our journey.

Tacked onto one of the leaf walls of Chief Gideon Buka's house was a picture torn out of a magazine showing Chris Evert playing tennis at Wimbledon. Gideon's wife scurried around, shooing out the hens and berating the villagers who peered at us through the doorways and windows of the house. "You must not mind these people," said Gideon. "It is not often that white people come to Baraula. But next month, ten Peace Corps workers will come here to learn pidgin and custom cooking. We are digging a latrine for them, a place where they can sit down. I am sorry that it is not ready for you."

The subject of toilet arrangements in villages had become rather a tricky one to broach, because there were so many different systems. United Mission villages had tiny leaf outhouses built on stilts over the water. SDA villages had separate beaches for men and women. In an Anglican village I'd been told to "use any rock." Now, in Baraula village, for the first time we'd encountered the Christian Fellowship Church and, perhaps, a different set of lavatorial rules. Gideon's wife Mary accompanied me to the "custom toilet." We walked for ten minutes, past rows of pigs snuffling inside bamboo cages, to an area planted with bananas. Mary pointed along a narrow path that wound through the large green leaves and towards the lagoon. It led me to a long, exposed beach where, at any minute, a fisherman could paddle by in his dugout and find me with my pants down. Glumly, I returned to Mary, who looked surprised to see me back so soon.

We set up our tent under the shelter of a half-built house in the center of the village. From the rafters above us, shark fins were hung up to dry. Three rows of children sat silently watching us, as if we were on a stage, until it grew dark and houses began to glow with the soft light of kerosene lamps. Like the surrounding jungle, Baraula was far from quiet at night. Babies wailed themselves to sleep. Adults snored. Western pop music crackled from someone's radio. Around 3 A.M., I crept out of the tent and made my way by flashlight to the "custom toilet." On the path through the banana leaves, I narrowly avoided stepping on an eight-inch long centipede. The thought of these fearsome-looking creatures and the fever induced by their painful bite threatened to inhibit me yet again. Trying not to think about crocodiles, I waded into the ocean and did what had to be done as fast as possible.

Turquoise water faded to glacial blue around islands ringed with bright white sand and shaded with palms. Vonavona was the smallest of the three lagoons and the most idyllic. It was only a few hours' paddle from there to Munda, where we were due to catch the *Iuminau* back to Honiara.

We deliberately missed one sailing of the ferry and spent several days exploring the lagoon. News of our presence quickly spread, and men paddled to our campsites to trade with us for fish hooks. They brought lobsters with pink and green carapaces, shimmering reef fish, juicy watermelons, coconuts. One evening, a fisherman called Charlie stayed with us to share our feast. He carefully sucked the flesh off every fishbone, and he opted for the head of the lobster, considering it most odd that we should prefer the tail. While we ate, he told us of a place in the lagoon where the remains of former chiefs and the spoils of headhunting days were kept. Intrigued, we asked him how to get there, but he shook his head.

"Skull Island is a *tambu* place," he warned. "If you go alone you will fall sick and die. The chief of Mandou Island must take you."

Charlie relayed the news of our interest in Skull Island to the chief, who sent his eldest son, Pinto, to accompany us there. After agreeing on a custom fee of twenty dollars Solomon, we set off with him across the lagoon. Pinto's dugout was extremely leaky, and he baled it with his feet while paddling at a furious rate, his arms working like a pair of pistons. Struggling to keep up, we followed him to a tiny, windswept outcrop of volcanic rock on the edge of the outer reef. On its far side, crashing waves sent spray high into the air. Anchoring on the lee side, we took a few steps to the heart of the island, where the undergrowth had been cleared away and a cairn built. I'd expected to see, at most, perhaps a dozen skulls. But there were scores of them, scattered over the cairn, tucked into its crevices, lying around it on the ground. Their crania were veined with fine moss and lichen, their eye sockets spun with spiders' webs and crawling with plant roots. With them lay arm bones, leg bones, ribs, an old clay pipe, a shark's tooth. Some of the skulls were disquietingly small, some had the lower jaw missing. All of them appeared to look back at us with steady, quizzical gazes. Pinto picked up one of the skulls on the ground and shoved it between two rocks.

"I can touch, but not you," he warned. "Once, a white man came here, put his cigarette between the jaws of a skull and took a photo. Soon after, he died of the three-day malaria." Cerebral malaria—the deadliest kind.

With renewed respect, I peered at the carved wooden chest on the top of the cairn. It was overgrown with pink and gray lichen, and inside it were a dozen more skulls lying on a pile of clamshells, the traditional currency of the Solomons.

"Before the missionaries came, this is where we put our chiefs' heads," said Pinto. "My great grandfather is in here. My grandfather is over there."

He pointed through the scrub vegetation to a gravestone and cross roughly engraved with the inscription: "Devito Vino. December 23 1986." Standing on it was a grimy glass jar containing a few plastic flowers, while all around colorful blossoms grew on trees and bushes.

"Whose . . . how . . . I mean . . . these skulls . . . ." Pinto waited patiently as I struggled to form my question. "Where did they come from?" I finally managed.

"Mostly from Isabel Province," he said. "Our people took the men's heads and brought back the fair-haired women as slaves."

"We're going to Isabel Province," I told him.

"Not many people left there," he said.

As the return journey to Honiara was by night, and rain was forecast, we decided to treat ourselves to one of the *Iuminau*'s two cabins. In relation to elsewhere on the boat, at first glance it appeared rather luxurious, with large windows, two single beds, a writing desk and a bathroom. On closer inspection it was less appealing. Brown cockroaches clung to the yellow walls, the sheets were stained and the bathroom was grimy and festooned with pubic hair. At least, we thought, we could both sleep without worrying about the safety of our boat and baggage, and we stretched out on one of the beds. Half an hour later, the first intercom announcement woke us. From the speaker above our heads a strident voice yelled that as the weather was rough and we were heading into open ocean, we should secure all our goods on deck and take particular care to not let our "pikininies rollem off." Soon the boat was pitching about, and the bathroom door was repeatedly swinging open and banging shut. Cockroaches began dropping on us from the ceiling, and a crunching, rustling noise started up in one corner of the room. The noise came closer, moved past the bed and over to another corner. Flicking on the light, we saw that a plastic bag and some paper had been removed from the wastepaper bin by the door and stuffed into a hole in the wall.

"It's only a rat," mumbled Dag, switching off the light and pulling the sheet over our heads.

Throughout the night the rat busied itself around us. We woke to discover it had stuffed several pieces of paper into its nest,

Hunted Heads 49

chewed on one of my notebooks, munched through a waterproof bag, and snacked on Dag's T-shirt, leaving it with seven holes, each with distinctive teeth marks.

As we approached the island of Guadalcanal, and Honiara, I sat in bed and watched Dag getting dressed. He sported a patchy tan and a scruffy beard, and three weeks of fish and coconuts had helped replace much of the weight he'd lost during his illness. As he shook his sun-bleached mop of hair to dislodge any errant cockroaches, and pulled on a pair of grimy shorts and a rat-chewed shirt, it struck me that he looked happier than he had for ages.

6

Island Life

"I didn't recognize you!" cried the clerk at Honiara's shipping office. "You look so healthy!"

When we told him of our plan to go to Isabel Province, his face fell. "No tourists go there! There are no roads, no hotels! You will be bored."

We assured him we needed neither roads nor hotels. In our kayak, we planned to explore the entire southwest coast of Santa Isabel, the longest of all the Solomon Islands, wend our way through the archipelago of islets at its western end and cross the Manning Strait to Choiseul Province.

"There's a boat scheduled to sail for Santa Isabel in two days," he told us. "But departure time could be brought forward from anything between one to thirty-six hours."

"How will we know?" we asked.

He shrugged. "Listen to the radio. Or keep an eye on the boat. When smoke comes from the funnels, go aboard."

The yellow funnels of *Ligomo V* belched out black smoke at nine that night, twenty-four hours ahead of schedule. A small wooden cargo boat with a ten-degree list, it was half the size of the *Iuminau,* and twice as basic. After we had spent a sleepless night steaming across a mercifully calm Solomon Sea, a lifeboat took us ashore at the south end of Santa Isabel Island.

As the *Ligomo V* chugged away, we assembled the kayak feeling hot, tired and very alone. All day we paddled northwest along a rugged, exposed coastline. White sandy bays alternated with black beaches and jungle-covered cliffs. The kayak creaked and bent in the steady swell, and Dag chose this time to tell me that he'd left our emergency locator unit and VHF radio in Honiara.

"I figured," he said blithely, "that there would be no one out here to rescue us, so it wasn't worth taking them along."

During the morning, huge gray clouds glowered at us, then around noon deluged us with torrential rain. As we passed a rocky offshore islet, hundreds of frigate birds rose up in a huge, wheeling spiral. Blue kingfishers flashed past us, and enormous butterflies with wings brown on one side and brilliant blue on the other flapped lazily by. In midafternoon we rounded a steep headland, where the water was made sloppy by rebounding waves. Beyond it, dwarfed by the steep mountainsides rising above it, was a village.

A crowd gathered on the beach, and several people splashed into the water and pulled the boat ashore with us still sitting in it. A gray-haired bare-breasted woman smoking a pipe reached into my cockpit and began pulling out bags and passing them to children.

"Where are they going?" I nervously muttered to Dag as the children, with his camera cases balanced on their heads, disappeared behind leaf houses. I needn't have worried. The people of Santa Isabel are renowned for their hospitality, and in every village there is a leaf hut which is left empty and ready for any dignitaries who may pass through. Waiting for us on the steps of Kilokaka's guest hut, with all our baggage neatly piled behind them, were the village organizer, James, and his small grandson. James told us that over the past few months only two people had stayed in the hut.

"A government official," he said. "And a health worker."

"Any white people in kayaks?" I asked.

"No white people," he replied. "Not since three years."

Solemnly, he accepted the tobacco and fish hooks we gave him, and encouraged his grandson to take the balloon we held out.

"I will bring you taro to eat," he said.

"We have our own food," I quickly told him. "But if anyone has fruit, we have things to trade for it."

First a woman arrived with an armful of papayas. When we

offered sewing needles in return, she shook her head.

"Balloon," she insisted.

Next came a spindly old man holding a huge machete in one hand and a thick stalk heavy with green, hard bananas in the other.

"We can't take those along," I muttered to Dag.

"We have to," he muttered back. "The poor fellow just cut them down from his garden."

He handed the old man some stainless steel fish hooks, which were scrutinized, then handed back.

"Balloons," he said.

Another woman brought pineapples, a man came with coconuts, children rolled oranges across the floor, someone offered eggs, and soon there was a noisy crowd of people around the door and a pile of food that was already too much for us to carry in the kayak. And everyone wanted balloons.

When darkness came, the women and children hurried home, but a group of men stayed to "story" and questioned us about life in Canada and England until past midnight. After what seemed like minutes of sleep, we were startled awake by loud drumming a few feet away from our heads. The hut next door was the church, and outside it, in the predawn light, the pastor was summoning the faithful to prayer by furiously banging two wooden sticks on a slit drum. Dag immediately got up, but I stayed under our bedsheet, sure that the noise would stop at any second. It went on for half an hour. At six o'clock, I was about to drift off to sleep again when I had the strong sense of being watched. Opening one eye, I saw three blond heads sticking through a hole in the bamboo floor. Directly beneath me, a dozen more small bodies were sitting cross-legged on the sand, staring up through the slats.

"Wefelas go lukim haus bilong yu?" asked the bravest of the three heads. "Can we visit your house?"

Taking my groan as an assent, within seconds the children had swarmed around me. While I faked sleep, they examined my scalp for lice. Presently they grew bored. I sat up, rummaged through our bag of trade items and found a balloon for them. They solemnly passed it around, then handed it back. I blew it up.

"Yu ple olgeta long balloon," I told them. "Play together with the balloon."

I gave a quick demonstration of patting it to keep it in the air. They filed out in silence, then erupted into delighted yelps, and I was able to dress in privacy while the balloon game went around the house. Inevitably, there was a loud pop! followed by a long, tense silence. A child appeared in the doorway. "Balloon gud no more," he told me in a small, frightened voice.

"No problem," I said.

"No problem?"

"No problem."

For the rest of the day the village echoed with the children's repeated cries of "No problem! No problem!"

I found Dag outside the church, admiring a man's pet baby opossum.

"Im bite?" he was asking.

"Im no bite," its owner assured him, and, as if to prove him wrong, the opossum promptly sunk its teeth into Dag's index finger. Another man appeared, pulling a tiny wild pig on a vine lead. He thrust the loudly squealing animal into Dag's arms.

"What's going on?" I asked.

"I told them I trained as a vet," he explained.

The next exhibit was a baby flying fox. It was hanging upside down from a length of bamboo, its face hidden beneath the soft, velvety skin that was strung between its long fingers and wrapped like wings around its body.

"Im *kaikai*," said its owner, poking it awake. "It's food."

The wings unfolded to reveal a furry black body with a pointed face, devilish ears and popping brown eyes. The bat yawned, opening wide a pink mouth lined with tiny, sharp teeth. Then it stretched out its "wings" and had a good scratch with the hooked end of an index finger.

"He's just like you in the mornings," I told Dag.

"I've got an idea," he said.

I didn't have to ask what it was.

"It's not possible—" I began.

"He could hang from the mast!" Dag said. "Look, he's already tame."

"Yufelas laikim?" asked the bat's owner. "Do you like him?"

"Wefelas laikim tumas!" enthused Dag.

"Yufelas taikim!" the owner offered.

"We can't take him," I said firmly.

"But he's so sweet," coaxed Dag, and he lifted the bat from the bamboo and attached it to my arm. Placing one claw over another, it started to make its way towards my armpit.

"Dag, please get it off."

"We could take him back to Canada! We've got a perfect house for him. He'd be a wonderful pet."

"Don't be ridiculous, we can't drag this thing around with us."

The bat, having discovered that my armpit wasn't a cave, had stretched up one long finger and hooked its claw into my hair.

"Get it off!"

"All right, all right," grumbled Dag, disentangling the baby bat.

"Sori tumas," he regretfully told its amused owner. "Misis bilong mi no laikim."

Although villages along the coast were few and far between, and without road or telephone connection, news of our journey traveled up the coast ahead of us. Some days later, when we arrived at Samasodu, the village organizer was waiting for us on the beach. "We are expecting you," John Selwyn said. "Your house is ready. Tonight there is a nativity play and you will be our special guests."

In the village meeting hall, banana leaf streamers hung from the tin roof, and patched sheets and sulus were pegged on to a rope to act as stage curtains. The audience sprawled over mats, babies slept on their mothers' backs, toddlers staggered around and tripped over sleeping dogs. Outside, the sky was star-filled, palms rustled in the warm breeze and the sound of breaking waves drifted over from the shore. Beneath the curtains, which didn't manage to reach the ground, a dozen pairs of bare black feet were hurrying about. The headmaster appeared, set two kerosene lamps at either side of the stage, then stood between them, wringing his hands.

"Mi sori long disfela drama," he began. "I'm sorry about this play."

Unctuously, he explained that he'd had to go to Honiara for a meeting, his return had been delayed and so he'd had little time to write and direct the play, or supervise the making of the costumes. The curtains were pulled back to reveal a girl and boy dressed in white sheets. Both looked uneasy. The boy had a pair of cardboard wings tacked to his back and he clutched a piece of paper.

"Angel Gabriel is come to Mary as a messenger from God!" announced the headmaster.

Gabriel began reading in a monotone from his notes, "Do not be afraid. Mary you have found favor. With the Lord you will be with child. And give birth to a son. And you are to give him the name Jesus."

Mary stared ahead, unblinking. "How will this be. Since I am a virgin," she said.

The headmaster paced up and down in front of the stage, wringing his hands. Gabriel cleared his throat and continued.

"Even Elizabeth your relative. Is going to have a child in her old age. And she who was said to be barren. Is in her sixth month for nothing is impossible with God."

A long silence ensued, while Gabriel and the Virgin Mary looked increasingly panic-stricken.

"Curtains!" hissed the headmaster, and the sulus and bed-sheets were jerked shut. Gabriel, minus his wings, and the Virgin came and stood in front of the stage.

"Joseph and Mary!" announced the headmaster. "No room at the inn!"

The solemn couple walked up and down in front of the curtains, while behind it ten pairs of feet belonging to the choir huddled together.

"Silen nie, holy nie," the choir began singing in soft uncertain voices, "all is cam, all is brie."

On reaching the familiar chorus, the voices let rip.

"SLEEEEP in HE-venly PEAS!" they screeched. "SLEEE-EEEP IN HE-VENLY PEAS."

When the carol was over, Mary and Joseph ducked behind the curtain. There was some angry muttering, the feet shuffled back and forth, then the curtain was yanked back to reveal a puzzled choir, Mary and Joseph kneeling either side of an empty box and three boys wearing cardboard crowns standing uncertainly at the side of the stage.

"Because I was in Honiara," the headmaster explained to the audience, "I had no time to teach the words of 'These Three Kings' or to make a baby Jesus."

Someone at the front of the audience volunteered a baby, but the frazzled headmaster rejected it.

"Come on, kings!" he said crossly, and in silence they shuffled over to the empty box and stared reverently down into it. The curtains closed for the last time.

"The drama is over," said the headmaster. "Sorry that we didn't have time to prepare more, but I was in Honiara."

Samasodu was the first village we'd visited that had running water. Down at the standpipe next morning, I washed our breakfast pots alongside a group of women who were scrubbing their already shining saucepans with sand. One of them grabbed my small, sooty kettle and set about it with a vengeance, while her friend went my for my frying pan. Fearing for its nonstick lining, I tried to tactfully dissuade her, but she carried on, tut-tutting about what she presumed to be stubborn stains.

"What is the purpose of your journey?" she inquired.

We'd been asked this question a hundred times already, and I still hadn't found a satisfactory answer. The concept of seeking adventure, and of taking time off work to do so, was alien in a place where people's lives revolved around the basics of survival. While I was still casting around for an explanation, she fired another question at me.

"And is it true that you left all your children at home?"

"I have no children," I told her.

She was stunned by this news, and I took the chance to gently pry the frying pan from her fingers. To cheer her up, I asked, "How many children do you have?"

"Five," she said. "But only three are with me. My sister is barren so I gave her my two youngest. "

She thought for a moment. "You must ask your wantoks for some of their children!" she pronounced.

I tried to imagine how my brothers and sisters-in-law would react to such a demand, or how Dag would feel about one of my boisterous nephews and nieces moving in with us. I was about to explain that adoption in my part of the world was far less casual than in hers, but she was so obviously satisfied with the solution she'd found to my dilemma that I thought better of it.

After Samasodu there were fifty miles of uninhabited coastline to the next village, Kia, on the northern tip of Santa Isabel. We paddled beyond the outer reefs, crossing them when necessary with a wish and a prayer that a rogue wave wouldn't decide to dump us onto the coral and wreck the kayak. And we kept our fingers crossed that the clement weather we were enjoying would stay with us. Through calm, crystal clear water, sharks cruised by us, curious but unobtrusive. Dolphins leaped up into the sunlight or swam on their backs right next to the boat, showing us their bright white bellies. And turtles popped their heads up, taking in gulps of air.

One evening, we camped on a black sand beach which appeared to have been chewed by an earth mover. These were the tracks of giant leatherback turtles: at this time of year they came ashore at night to lay their eggs in the sand. After dark, we walked along the beach, straining our eyes and ears. Soon, we heard a deep grunting. We crept forward, Dag turned on the flashlight, and we jumped back in alarm at what its beam picked out. The turtle was at least half a ton in weight; the top of her ridged shell stood four feet from the ground and her splayed front flippers, tip to tip, were eight feet across. But there was nothing to fear from her: she was so engrossed in her egg-laying preparations that I doubt she even noticed our presence.

Using her back flippers like scoops, she spent an hour digging a narrow hole in the sand. When the hole was two feet deep, she began to lay her eggs. They were surprisingly small, like soft golf balls. As they fell out of her, her grunts changed to long groans, and big gelatinous tears oozed from her eyes. It took her half an hour to lay about a hundred eggs. She rested for a while, panting as if trying to regain some strength. Then, with the utmost tenderness, she gently patted sand over the eggs and began filling in the hole. By now, her groans must have been those of pure exhaustion, but her work wasn't over yet. Shuffling sideways, she dug two more holes and filled them in as decoys for the predatory lizards. Finally, her work completed, she turned and lumbered back to the water. The waves broke over her shell, and she was gone. All night, turtles emerged from the surf like huge mythical creatures, and all night we stayed up and watched them. The last ones retreated to their own element just before dawn broke. We managed an hour of sleep before the sun rose and started beating into the tent. When we crawled outside, it was to discover four-foot-long monitor lizards up and down the beach, busily digging for their breakfast.

The lack of sleep made us grumpy for the rest of the day. We paddled past long stretches of inhospitable swamp and mangroves, and through a muddle of steep, rocky islets where the air was still and unbearably hot. I constantly had to shift around in my seat to ease the discomfort of a fungal infection and a few salt-water sores. I remembered the advice of a friend in Canada, who had said that when the going got rough I should try creative visualization techniques.

Dutifully, I imagined myself as a hermit crab, curled up in my cool, dark shell. It didn't work. Then I imagined myself lying between crisp linen sheets in a shuttered room. That didn't work either.

"Let's stop soon," I suggested.

"Good idea, can you suggest somewhere?" Dag snapped.

"You've got the map, doesn't it show any beaches?"

"I've been looking at this map all day, why don't you take over that side of things?"

By now, we'd perfected the art of paddling and squabbling at the same time. Dag hurled his wrath at my back; I hurled mine at the ocean. "For heaven's sake, just tell me if there are any beaches about!"

"No, there aren't."

"What are we going to do?"

"I don't know, why don't you make a suggestion for a change?"

"What's the point, we always do what you want anyway!"

The row was interrupted by a piercing whistle. We turned to see a man waving to us from one of the rocky islets.

"Hello! Helloooo! Over here!" he called, and guided us into a small bay concealed by mangroves, where an open-fronted house stood on stilts over the water.

Kora Islet was very different from the pristine Melanesian villages we'd visited so far. Plastic kerosene bottles floated among the mangrove roots. Beneath a washing line, clothes were trampled into the mud. Pieces of corrugated iron and firewood lay around. A path of coconut husks had been partly built and then abandoned. Next to a ramshackle kitchen hut, smoked sea slugs, or beche-de-mer, lay scattered over the ground, and scruffy chickens scratched in the dirt. But Victor Thagramana warmly welcomed us, pushing aside heaps of clothing and bedding, and laying a mat for us to sit on by the open doorway of the tiny house. He told us that he was a police bandmaster in Honiara, and that Kora Islet was his custom land. He, his Polynesian wife Christina and their daughter Jemima were here for the Christmas holidays, visiting Christine's mother, Rhonda, who lived in this, the only settlement on Kora.

"In Honiara, I work hard, earn money, spend it all on food and rent," said Victor. "Here, I live freely. I eat cassava from the garden and fish from the sea. If I need money I sell a little beche-de-mer or copra. I enjoy island life. I forget about work!"

While Victor rejoiced over forgetting about work, the women of his family were out catching dinner. Towards late afternoon they paddled their dugout back from the reef, singing Polynesian songs in three-part harmony. Victor's wife and mother-in-law were portly women with halos of frizzy hair. His nineteen-year-old daughter Jemima had a lithe body the color of nutmeg, covered only by a casually knotted sulu which kept slipping from her breasts. Straight black hair framed her face and cascaded to her waist. Around her forehead was a garland of fresh turmeric, and in one hand she held the afternoon's catch of several large trevally.

After a dinner of fish and rice, Dag presented Victor with some tobacco.

"We have had no tobacco for one week!" Victor cried. "Now there are smiles everywhere!"

Using school exercise-book paper, he rolled up several fat cigarettes, handing the first to his mother-in-law. Then he produced a large battered kettle filled with *kalevi*, a strong grog made from fermented coconut palm sap.

"It has to be finished tonight!" he announced gleefully, passing me a half coconut shell brimming with the opaque, slightly fizzy liquid. "Otherwise it burns holes in the kettle!"

It was pleasant stuff, but strong, and after two shellfuls I was yawning. Leaving Dag and Victor to work their way through the kettle, I helped the women to hang up mosquito nets from the ceiling of the house and to lay out mats and sheets beneath them. Soon I was drifting off to sleep. Rhonda and Christina snored wheezily, a beche-de-mer exploded on the smoking rack in the cook house, and, below me, water slapped around the mangrove roots.

"This is island life!" I heard Victor cry. "You drink, fall down, sleep, get up, fish!"

At dawn, a hand lifted a corner of our mosquito net and slid in a glass jar containing several freshly picked wild orchids. Minutes later the net was lifted again and a thermos flask and two plastic cups were pushed beneath it. Inside the flask was a hot drink made from lemon grass, water and sugar.

"We're in heaven," said Dag.

By the time we had dismantled the mosquito net and rolled up the mat, Jemima had arrived with our breakfast: Hard Navy biscuits, homemade coconut jam liberally peppered with ants, and three boiled eggs. Dag peeled off one of the egg shells, releasing a powerful, sulfurous smell and revealing a well-developed embryo.

"I can't eat that!" I whispered to Dag.

He, however, can eat almost anything. He rummaged around in our food bag for a bottle of soy sauce, and tipped it liberally over the peeled egg.

"Don't!" I said, watching in horror as he put the whole egg into his mouth and, with a grim expression on his face, began determinedly chewing. He swallowed, reached for the water bottle and drank steadily from it for half a minute. Then he slipped the remaining eggs into the pockets of his shorts.

"I'll be back soon," he said, and sauntered off towards the mangroves.

A little later Jemima sidled over to me.

"You want a swim?" she asked me, meaning did I want to wash.

Hitching her sulu over her breasts, she led me along the coconut path. It turned into a muddy trail and wound through huge ferns to where a stream trickled out of the rock and formed a small, murky pool. Scattered around it were broken plastic bowls, bits of laundry soap, and more trodden-in washing. Jemima squatted down by the pool and trailed her long fingers across the surface of the water. I hunkered down next to her, uncertain of what I was supposed to do. She looked from side to side, her dark eyes searching the dense foliage around us. Then she put her head close to mine.

"Your husband went to mangroves," she whispered. "I saw."

"Yes," I whispered back, casting around for an explanation of the egg disposal.

"He makes his toilet on land?" she asked. "Or sea?"

"Sometimes in the sea," I told her. "Sometimes on land."

"Land is dangerous!" she hissed. "There are *velas* around here!"

We'd heard a lot about velas, the magicians said to get their power by murdering the person they love the most. I'd been warned that a local girl could make Dag fall in love with her by stealing a hair from his head and taking it to a vela. We'd heard of velas with crooked fingers who could kill us by putting our spirits in a basket, and velas who could steal our footprints and possess us. Now Jemima had news of a different type.

"If you make your toilet on land, the vela can take a piece of it and use it to put bad magic on you. But the sea has a good spirit and if your toilet is in it the velas cannot touch it."

"Where are these velas?" I asked.

Her eyes skittered about. "Everywhere! Some places are not blessed and evil spirits live in the trees."

Above us, the leaves rustled, and I looked up and met the gaze of a large green monitor lizard clinging to a branch.

"We'll make our toilet in the sea," I promised her, and we hurried back down the path towards the sunlight.

Days slid lazily by. Each afternoon we paddled with the women to the reef to fish and to dive for beche-de-mer. On the way home we stopped at mangrove swamps to collect firewood. Once, we snorkeled around the submerged remains of a Second World War fighter plane. It was surprisingly intact, and lay on one wing in twenty feet of sun-dappled water. I tried to imagine the gunfire, the flames, the pilot's fear as the plane went down. But staghorn coral grew from the rudder, angel fish fluttered through the portholes, a moray eel curled around a machine gun mounting and all echoes of violence seemed long, long gone.

In the evenings we sat under the stars, drinking kalevi and swapping stories, then retired to the house to sleep with the mosquito nets billowing around us in the warm breeze.

"Stay for Christmas!" said Victor one night. "Stay longer! We'll build you a house!"

It was perfectly possible to imagine canceling the rest of our trip around the world and spending months on Kora Islet. One morning, we realized that if we didn't leave right away, we never would. After a last breakfast, Jemima slipped frangipani garlands over our heads and presented us with a jar of her ant-peppered jam. We gave the family fishing lures and line, the rest of the tobacco, a hat, and a T-shirt. They squeezed into their dugout canoe and paddled with us to the outer reef, singing Polynesian songs of farewell. By the time we crossed the reef, I was so awash with tears that the open ocean ahead was a blur. Behind us, the Thagramanas floated in their canoe, singing until we were out of sight. Their sweet harmonies gradually faded away, but once Victor's shout rang out, loud and clear.

"Remember island life! Come back to us one day!"

7

A Reward

After Kora, the large village of Kia seemed almost urban. Leaf houses crowded the narrow shoreline, and outside its several well-stocked stores groups of young men, heavily stoned on betel, hung around with ghetto-blasters glued to their ears.

"Oh mi Anita!" went the popular song of the time. "Mi bilong yu! Yu breakin' heart bilong mi! Mi kam back again, mi hope yu wait mi!"

In one of the stores, where we replenished our dwindling food supplies, we met a woman called Edith who had lived in Ottawa for one year and was soon to leave for Melbourne to complete her B.S. in nursing.

"I go to foreign countries to learn the latest methods," she told us, "then I come back here to a ward full of patients who think they are bewitched. Sometimes I wonder if my training was a waste of time."

She invited us into her parents' house, where her father was boiling fish heads over a kerosene stove while his wife grated coconut.

"I came to check on my customary land and my parents," said Edith. "I will go back to Honiara tonight or tomorrow, whenever the boat comes, so they make food for my journey. See how hard the island life is? No electricity, no running water. Working in the garden all day, then spending hours preparing food."

I asked her how she had felt when she first arrived in Canada.

"I was amazed! Like the people from Kia when they first go to

Honiara, like you when you came here. But then I got used to it. That is the problem, you get used to one thing, then you must change. Sometimes I think it would be better if I had stayed at home and not gone to secondary school and to college. My life is too confusing, I don't know where I belong."

The fish heads were left to boil over while Edith's father scrutinized our map. We told him of our plan to find a channel through the maze of islands north of Santa Isabel, then cross the Manning Strait, notorious for its currents and rip tides.

"Should we go through the channel when tide is high or low?" Dag asked.

"Yesss," answered Edith's father.

Dag tried again. "When is the best time to go through the channel?"

Edith's father scratched his head. "Tomorrow," he said.

Erratic currents led us astray, islets and bays not shown on our map appeared, and soon we were lost. Steep slopes towered above us, and the jungle pressed in, steamy and oppressive. As we searched for the channel, a series of alarming twists and turns took us into dead ends where huge tree roots grew from the water and vines hung in such tangles that we had to haul the boat through them. Thick prickly leaves ripped our skin and grabbed at our hair. The thought of crocodiles was never far away. Once, we got stuck among low overhanging branches, floating in shallow water infested by large stingrays with black tails and speckled backs that zoomed around the boat. It took hours of this torture before we found the channel, and by then our drinking water was worryingly low. Finally, towards evening, the steep jungle walls eased back, and we spied the open ocean. We were through. Just before the end of the channel we found a protected bay with a small beach, a rock bluff—and a stream! Unable to believe our good fortune we pulled ashore. As the day drew to a close and tiny bats started flitting around our heads, Dag fried cassava slices over a small fire while I washed myself in the stream. Our relief was too great for us to be concerned about the rushing sounds of the tide rips out in the Manning Strait.

Four hours of fighting hard against strong currents and steep waves had their reward: the Arnavon Islands, a few uninhabited scraps of land, sculpted by wind and waves, in the middle of the Manning Strait. The island we chose as our home for a few days had a long, wedge-shaped beach, tapering to a point with the luminous blue sea curling around it on both sides. It was an impossibly pretty, romantic place, the desert isle of everyone's dreams. We stripped off our clothes, which were so stiff with salt they could practically stand up by themselves. There was no fear of causing offense with our nakedness—as far as the eye could see there was no sign of human life, not even a boat on the horizon or the tail of a jet in the sky.

Surrounding the island was a coral reef made intriguing by exposure to currents, and untouched by humans. At the edge of the reef there was a dizzying drop-off, a sheer cliff where the shafts of sunlight were swallowed up by the shadowy depths, and where parrot and grouper fish of an immense size advanced curiously upon these two strange creatures invading their domain. I only peeked over the edge of the cliff, preferring to snorkel in the security of the shallows and their pretty coral gardens. But Dag spent hours exploring it, using a weight belt, flippers and great lungfuls of air to dive deep. Spooked by the size of the fish, however, he never bothered to take out his spear gun.

"I'm worried," he said, "that *they* might decide to take *me* home to their wives for supper."

When I wasn't snorkeling, I did little but move from one shady spot to another. Scattered over the sand around me were weathered gray coconuts, some sprouting fresh green shoots topped with tender ribbed leaves. Hermit crabs busily crawled about, and through the bushes I could see gawky megapode birds, which laid their large eggs in the warm sand and then abandoned them to incubate on their own. The branches above me swayed as red parrots hopped about them, pecking at flowers and scolding each other. Kingfishers dive-bombed into the water, white cockatoos swooped by. Large bugs, like deer flies, constantly hovered around me, attracted by my sticky skin. It was too hot to do much but lie back and think. Often, my thoughts would concern Dag, swimming off the reef. I'd consider the possibility of him being attacked by a shark. What if he came back with some terrible gaping wound? We had suture materials with us, but he was the one with a medical background. What if he simply didn't come back? Through binoculars I scanned a distant reef, where perfectly sculpted waves seemed to pause and show off their smooth green bellies before breaking in a surge of white foam. And beyond, the currents of the Manning Strait met with wind and kicked up waves that made the horizon look bumpy and blurred. Where, in this expanse of sea and sky, would I go for help? Just as panic would begin to creep up on me, I'd see Dag's head as he came up for air, the sunlight glinting on his body as it curved through the water, and finally his flippers sliding beneath the surface.

Our food supplies were so low that they rattled around in the bottom of the once bulging waterproof bag. One night we cooked up some taro leaves that we'd brought from Kia. Although they were horribly wilted, we steamed them along with some grated coconut, and the result was quite tasty.

"They're very tender," commented Dag after his first bite. "I wonder why local people always cook them for so long."

As we each had a second bite, I suddenly remembered what I'd seen in the village cook houses.

"They boil—" I began, but Dag was already clutching at his neck, with his eyes a pair of bulging question marks.

"What's going on?" he croaked.

"They boil them—" I managed, before my throat seemed to close up and speaking became impossible. It was as if my esophagus had suddenly sprouted hundreds of burning, itching barbs. Terrifying thoughts flashed through my mind—of our windpipes being cut off, of us staggering around and slowly choking to death, of our bodies lying undiscovered for months. Gradually, I realized that, while not going away, the effects weren't getting any worse, and that we were both still breathing.

"You have to boil taro leaves twice," I finally managed to hoarsely whisper.

"Thanks for the tip," Dag rasped back.

Repairing our throats accounted for a good deal of our water supply; soon, we realized, we would have to get across the Manning Strait and over to the villages on Vaghena Island.

"We shouldn't linger here anyway, because bad weather could move in fast," said Dag. "Besides, we've got to find out about a ship from Vaghena back to Honiara. Our flight to Australia leaves in just over a week, you know."

I knew, but I didn't want to think about it.

8

Ships That Have Sailed

By noon the next day we'd completed the crossing of the Manning Strait and arrived in Kukutin, on the southwest side of Vaghena Island. Here we learned that the last ship to Honiara before Christmas had already sailed. In two days' time another ship was scheduled to leave for the capital from the port of Noro, on New Georgia Island, seventy miles across New Georgia Sound.

"Let's paddle to Noro," I suggested.

Dag looked at me in horror. "Are you kidding?"

"We can set out before dawn," I insisted.

"What if bad weather moves in? We'd be on open ocean for forty miles. Do you realize how committing such a long crossing is? Have you gone nuts?"

Obviously I had.

"We're fit and acclimatized," I said breezily. "It will nicely round off our time in the Solomons."

"It might round us off as well," said Dag sardonically, but I could tell he was pleased that, for a change, it was me taking the initiative, me pushing for challenge, me coming up with a crazy idea.

Vaghena Island's original Melanesian population was wiped out last century by disease and head-hunting. Thirty years ago, Micronesians began moving from the overpopulated Gilbert Islands to Vaghena, where they established three villages, of which Kukutin is the largest. Unlike Melanesians, the Gilbertese people don't have a tradition of self-sufficient gardening, so on

Vaghena their main livelihood comes from the abundance of seafood in the surrounding waters. Recently, a Taiwanese company had made some investments in Vaghena Island. It equipped fishermen with engines for their canoes, it installed generator-run freezers in the village and it made contracts to buy up the harvests of giant clams and crayfish, which it regularly collects in high-speed boats. Vaghena, a remote island with no roads, telephones, electricity or running water, suddenly became a consumer society.

In Kuktutin's narrow river mouth we'd nosed the boat through slimy water strewn with floating litter and fish carcasses. Tied up next to a small bridge was a large and modern motorboat with the name *Mr. Muscle* crudely stenciled on its prow. Lounging on deck, chewing gum and listening to a pop version of "Jingle Bells" on a ghetto-blaster, was a Taiwanese fish trader in blue jeans and a tight T-shirt. When he told us that we'd missed the ferry to Honiara, we asked about the possibility of camping in the village.

"You must talk to Henry," he said.

On a mat spread over the crushed coral floor of his kitchen hut, Henry sat cross-legged and contemplative. He was a squarely built man with sad almond-shaped eyes and thick gray hair combed back from a wide forehead. He wore only a towel, wrapped sulu-style around his waist, and a large digital wristwatch. Scrawny chickens pecked among the coral, searching for crumbs, and if one came too close to Henry he swatted it with the palm leaf he was using as a fan. His wife, June, who was also big, wide-faced and towel-wrapped, was busily feeding wood into the oil drum cooking stove and heaping food from blackened pots on to metal plates. Soon the mat was covered with dishes: sweet potato, rice, corned beef with onion, lobster, fresh bread and margarine. One of the chickens managed a few brave pecks at the rice before Henry's wrath descended on it, and it ran, squawking loudly, right through the plate of corned beef and out the door.

"Eat," commanded Henry.

He was terribly concerned about our plans to cross to Noro, and from time to time he rubbed his eyes with the back of his hand and gave a deep sigh.

"Please do not leave on this terrible journey," he said.

In Kukutin, Henry was a man of influence. He owned a general store, he had a house with a corrugated iron roof and a generator, and he ran the village cinema. After lunch, we went to his store and bought packets of a savory snack called Cheese Twisties, tubes of frozen fruit cordial called Ice Blocks and tickets for the afternoon video show. A video! After two months spent on isolated beaches and in traditional villages, with our only power sources a flashlight, a kerosene lamp and the fuel for our cooking stove, this seemed sophistication beyond belief. We followed Henry into the back room of the store. Its concrete floor was spread with cracked linoleum and the windows were covered with sheets of corrugated iron. Henry insisted we sit on the only two chairs, amidst a jumble of old oil cans, sacks of rice, coils of ropes and empty cardboard boxes. The audience—men leaning against the walls, teenagers and small children sprawling on the floor—was focused on a large television screen, across which Cher was dancing about in a black leotard with strategically placed holes.

"If I could turn back time!" she sang, thrusting out her pelvis.

On broad, bare feet, Henry plodded up to the VCR and pressed a button, causing Cher to instantly disappear. In the sudden hush we could hear the steady thumping of the generator. He slotted a cartridge into the machine, and the afternoon feature began. It was a Chinese film, its plot made incomprehensible by the lack of dubbing or subtitles. Nonetheless, the crowd was agog and roared its approval of the sword fights, gory stabbings and decapitations.

"Let's go," I whispered to Dag, but he was working his way through a packet of Cheese Twisties without taking his eyes off the screen. He didn't seem to notice when I crept away through a side door.

Outside, a sour smell rose from the river. It was midafternoon, the hottest part of the day, and men lay about in the shade of houses raised several feet off the ground on stilts. On the gray sand, a group of women sat weaving bright green sago palm leaves into sections for a thatched roof. Two girls walked by carrying between them a bamboo pole with a bucket of water suspended from it. Naked children played in the dust, flicking rubber bands to see who could get them to go furthest. A hen and several chicks wandered into the store and were shooed out, clucking and flapping. The peaceful scene was broken when a motorized canoe roared into the mouth of the river. Its driver cut the engine and began yelling, causing a general rousing among the sleeping men.

"What's happening?" I asked one of the women.

"They have caught big turtles," she answered.

It took two men to slaughter a turtle. Together, they heaved the creature out of the canoe and onto its back. One man stood on the turtle's front flippers to immobilize it. The other used a long, sharp knife to cut around the edge of the shell. Thick blood oozed and then flowed freely, turning the water bright red. The man slid the knife beneath the skin of the belly and lifted it clean away, revealing pulsating innards. The turtle was still alive. Helplessly, it raised its head and waved its back flippers. The man put down his knife, plunged his hands inside the turtle and began disemboweling it. I closed my eyes and thought of the sleeping turtles we'd seen while snorkeling, the small turtles that often surfaced for air in front of the kayak, the giant leatherback turtles we'd watched laying their eggs. When I reopened my eyes, one man was wrenching off the turtle's flippers, and the other was scraping out its shell.

As soon as the afternoon video finished, Henry helped us unpack our boat, standing with us in the filthy river water. Then he and June carried our gear to their house and insisted we share their upstairs living area. Flimsy walls separated the space into four rooms furnished with mats and cardboard boxes. From one of these rooms some children, of which Henry seemed to have an indeterminate number, were cleared out to make way for us. We were shown the outside latrine and bath house, an impressive arrangement with a cement plinth for squatting on and a large tin bath filled with fresh water for washing. And, for the evening video show, in my honor Henry chose an English B movie about gang warfare in London.

The nighttime crowd was bigger than during the afternoon and included women, teenage girls and small babies. They watched white men chase around in cars, blow up safes, rob banks and shoot each other. It was such a bad copy that Dag and I could barely understand the dialogue; to everyone else in the room it must have been as incomprehensible and alien as the Chinese film earlier that day. When it was over and the lights went up, Henry padded over to us.

"There is a dancing practice in the village. The people are

preparing for Christmas. Would you like to see? My daughter Agatha will take you there."

In seconds we were transported from London's underworld to a tropical island, where fruit bats squabbled in the papaya trees and a balmy wind blew in from the sea. We followed Agatha along paths between thatch houses to the far end of the village, where an open-sided meeting house was packed with people. In the center, a group of ten men sat on the floor, drumming on upturned wooden boxes and leading the crowd in songs about village affairs, fishing and Jesus. At one end of the house, women were dancing. They wore T-shirts with slogans like "Surf City" or "Rock 'n Roll," grass skirts and frangipani garlands. In contrast to the exuberant singing, they danced with precise, perfectly timed movements of head, hands, arms and feet. Agatha was too busy questioning me to join them.

"Why don't you have any children? How long have you been married? What is your religion? Does it rain like this in your country?"

A sudden tropical storm had hit. Rain hammered on the corrugated iron roof and bounced off the ground outside. Shuffling inward, away from the open sides of the house, the crowd sang louder than ever. It was after ten o'clock when we returned to Henry's house, where the generator still thumped and electric lights blazed.

"Do not go on this journey," Henry pleaded over breakfast. "Stay here for Christmas."

We assured him it was something we were choosing to do, but he wouldn't be convinced.

"You are like my son and daughter. I am worried about you in your little boat."

All day, the generator thumped while we sat in Henry's house sorting through our gear. As we were shortly to fly out of the Solomon Islands, we wanted to lighten our luggage as much as possible. We heaped Henry with gifts: a weight belt for diving, fishing tackle, a fish grill and the rest of our trade items.

"It's not enough to repay your kindness," we insisted, but he accepted the gifts with a mixture of gratitude and profound concern. That night, he showed what he considered to be his best video, featuring a young Steve McQueen playing a half-Indian. It was a favorite of the audience, which cheered at the scene where

McQueen paddles a dugout canoe through a Louisiana swamp. As soon as the film finished we went to bed, needing a good rest before the long ocean crossing. We set our alarm for four o'clock, then settled down, expecting the lights and the noisy generator to go off at eleven, as they had the night before. But they stayed on, and on, and on. The thump of the generator reverberated through the floor of our room and rattled the walls. At 2 a.m., Dag got up to use the latrine. He found Henry sitting Buddhalike and surrounded by white feathers outside the kitchen hut, while his wife busied around inside it.

"Why are you up so late?" Dag asked him.

"We are cooking a chicken," said Henry.

For us, of course. With all our gifts, we had tipped the delicate balance of generosity, and now Henry felt in our debt and was anxious to repay us.

"Sleep now," he insisted. "Rest for your journey."

This was easier said than done. We dozed fitfully, and just before the alarm went off, we woke and sat bolt upright, convinced that the sun had risen and that we'd overslept. But then we heard the beat of the generator, and realized the light came from electric bulbs. Loud snoring told us that the whole family was now asleep. Stepping over the children on the veranda, we crept downstairs and over to where the boat was anchored. Minutes later we were joined by Henry, June and Agatha, who held our flashlights while we packed the boat.

"You do not have to go on this journey," said Henry. "You can stay with us for Christmas."

Repeating our gratitude, we said good-bye, and June handed us the chicken and warm, freshly baked bread.

The moon was already down, the night inky black and the sea so flat calm that it mirrored the stars, and we seemed to be paddling off into the sky itself. After ten minutes I turned around; the lights at Henry's house had finally been turned off, and it was as if Vaghena Island had never existed and our time there had been an illusion.

With dawn came a cloud cover that kept the morning cool and helped us to establish a steady paddling rhythm. Around eight o'clock huge cumulus clouds moved towards us, trailing veils of rain. But within minutes the sun came out, the clouds burned off and our shirts steamed dry. We stopped for breakfast:

peanuts, June's bread, and the ant and coconut jam we'd saved from Kora Island. Behind us, Vaghena was a faint line on the horizon. Far ahead, across an eerily calm expanse of cobalt water, we could see the peak of the volcanic island of Kolombangara. There were no birds in sight, no boats. Once again we were utterly alone, out in the Solomon Sea, this time not on a tiny island, but in a kayak.

It's one thing to paddle a few miles offshore—although being in striking distance of land is not necessarily a guarantee of safety, psychologically it has a most reassuring effect. But an open ocean crossing is quite another matter, especially when you reach the halfway point and turning back is no longer an option. By then, you are committed whether or not you like it, and you simply have to keep an eye on the compass, make one paddle stroke after the other and, if you're lucky enough to have good conditions, hope that they hold.

We had no storms to contend with, no cresting waves, no strong currents, no headwind. Unfortunately, there was no wind at all. The air was so still that it seemed as if the day was holding its breath, and heat seemed to hang from the sky like a heavy, damp curtain. At eleven we stopped for a lunch break and pulled out the unfortunate chicken which had been responsible for our lack of sleep the night before. Despite its unappetizing pale gray color, it was surprisingly tasty. We ate it with the salty Hard Navy biscuits we'd bought in Henry's store, and tossed the remains overboard. Then we considered a swim. We were paddling across a stretch of water where shark fishermen make big catches. They go out with rattles made of giant clam and half coconut shells strung onto thick vine, and shake these just below the surface of the water to summon up the sharks.

"Out there," Henry had warned us, "sharks are always watching and listening, and many things attract them."

Many things? Fingers, toes, legs, feet, chicken carcasses? All morning, such considerations had prevented me plopping into the water to cool down. When I'd needed to pee, I hung over the side of the kayak. But now, the urge to swim was becoming irresistible.

"Are sharks attracted to chicken bones?" I asked Dag, as casually as I could.

"No, but they are to pink shorts," he teased.

In we went. Although the water temperature was probably

around 82 degrees, compared to an air temperature in the 90s
and a humidity approaching 100 percent, it felt refreshingly cool.
We swam around and under the boat. Suddenly, from the corner
of my eyes, I saw a flash of something long and white. Part of my
brain instantly reminded me that the worst thing to do in the
vicinity of sharks is to splash about. But another, more dominant
part overrode this sensible advice and propelled me to the boat
and into the cockpit in a mad frenzy of flailing limbs.

"There's something in the water!" I yelled at Dag.

He was the picture of relaxation, floating on his back, his arms
behind his head, his chest puffed out to give him buoyancy.

"I saw it," he laconically replied. "It's a length of toilet paper. It
floated out of your shorts pocket."

At midday, when our skins were parched and encrusted with
salt, the sun began its serious torment. It bounced off the water
and onto my face and neck, making my hat and sunglasses practically useless. The heat became a physical entity. It lowered itself
onto us, it beat down on our heads and sucked the moisture from
our bodies. Wearing shirts became unbearable, so we took them
off, soaked our sulus in the ocean and draped them around our
shoulders. The gaps between our breaks became shorter. We
went into the water every hour, and then every forty-five minutes.
We stopped eating, and just drank liter after liter of water, grateful that we'd decided to carry so much with us. The color of the
sea and sky bleached out until the horizon was hard to distin-
guish and seemed to dance about before our eyes. My arms felt
as if they were no longer part of my body but some piece of
machinery which had been attached to me and programmed to
paddle and paddle and paddle . . .

During the afternoon, the islands of Kolombangara and New
Georgia gradually eased up from the horizon and began to loom
to the west and south. By six o'clock we could make out individual trees on the slopes of New Georgia, and it seemed we would
be there in minutes. We planned to find a beach, camp overnight
and set off at dawn for the last stretch to Noro. Now that the end
of the day was in sight, my arms became reattached to my torso
and my brain told me how very tired they were. The water
seemed to have become thick and viscous, and pushing a paddle
through it was a terrible effort. The sun slipped away in a blaze of
color, turning the clouds shrouding the summit of Kolomban-

gara a vivid orange. A school of dolphins surfaced and frolicked around us. Apart from a few flying fish, they were the only other living creatures we'd seen all day. Darkness began to settle, and still we hadn't reached our goal.

"I've heard of receding hairlines," Dąg groaned. "but never of receding coastlines!"

Slowly, slowly, we drew closer. The moon came up but played peek-a-boo behind a thin cloud cover forming across the sky. Ahead of us, the jungle-clad slopes of New Georgia Island were a dark, dense wall, eerily echoing with screams, whistles, pops and trills. A warm wind blew offshore, bringing with it the heavy scents of tropical flowers and damp earth. And the sound of breaking waves told us we were approaching a coral reef. We inched along, listening, peering through the darkness at the white foam of waves where we knew we couldn't cross the reef, and hoping to see dark patches of deeper water where perhaps we could. There were no dark patches. Behind me, Dag cursed.

"It's December twentieth," he said. "Tomorrow is summer solstice. We're arriving here at one of the lowest tides of the year."

"What shall we do?" I asked.

We both knew there was only one answer to that question, but neither of us wanted to voice it. The tide was dropping, we couldn't cross the reef, so we simply had to carry on.

Around ten o'clock, a new smell drifted to us from shore: burning wood. We saw a soft glow swinging through the darkness. Someone was walking along carrying a kerosene lamp. Listening keenly, we heard voices, and a dog barking. The proximity of somewhere to stop and rest was an unbearable thought.

"We couldn't go ashore there anyway," said Dag reassuringly. "The people would think we were ghosts. We'd scare them silly."

My vision was playing tricks. Kolombangara Island reared up from the sea like a gargantuan tidal wave. Lightning storms hurled dazzling, writhing snakes across the sky. Just before midnight, we decided that we were too tired to continue. Dropping a sea anchor to prevent the boat drifting, we wriggled down and folded our legs around all the bags of gear stowed beneath the deck. Although far from comfortable, we both fell instantly asleep. It was a short respite: three hours later we were awake again, feeling damp and shivery. But now there were two incentives to keep paddling: ahead was a faint glow of light which we presumed to be the port of Noro, and to the east, stars were beginning to fade from the sky.

Dawn was slow and unspectacular, just a gray light pushing away the last vestiges of the night. It found us paddling through a stretch of protected water between Kolombangara and New Georgia Islands, and fantasizing about soft white beaches. Alas, there were none in sight. As soon as the reef was safe to cross we headed over to New Georgia, where between thick jungle and the water there was a narrow coastal strip of sharp volcanic rock. I knew from experience that, in terms of somewhere to rest, this would be the equivalent of a bed of nails. But we were desperate to get out of the boat, even it was only to stand and stretch. As we came close to the shore, I thought my eyes were starting to play tricks again. The rocks appeared to be undulating. They were also making strange clicking sounds. Abruptly, Dag stopped paddling.

"No way," he said quietly, "am I getting out here."

Stretching from the shoreline to the forest wall was a deep, writhing layer of land crabs. There were thousands upon thousands of them, clambering and scuttling all over each other, four and five deep in places. Horrified and fascinated, we watched from a few yards offshore. Each crab had an egg sack on its lower abdomen, and when it scrambled down to the edge of the rocks it raised its pincers and wriggled its body in a comical hula dance, releasing a cloud of eggs into the water. Then it turned and fought its way back through the tide of oncoming crabs. The water was murky with eggs, and colorful fish were milling about, enjoying the feast. Once again, not wanting to voice the inevitable, I asked an unnecessary question.

"What shall we do?"

"Keep paddling," said Dag.

After a few miles, the crab layer thinned out and eventually disappeared. We anchored the boat and waded to shore, stepping gingerly over sharp rocks. We'd been at sea for twenty-five hours; our limbs were tired and stiff, our backsides raw and aching. Finding a patch of jungle that had been cleared and planted with taro and cassava, I lay down on a fallen log while Dag opened up our last can of tuna and spread it onto biscuits.

"We've got company," he said, and I looked up to see two small boys pulling a dugout canoe onto the shore. On bare feet, they walked across the sharp rock and sat down a short distance away, staring at us with wide eyes.

"How far is it to Noro?" we asked them.

"Two hours," they said.

"That means four," I predicted, and I was right.

When we clambered back into the boat I felt as cold as I had been during the night, and I longed for the sun to climb up into the sky and warm me. Which it soon did, and with a vengeance. Once again the day was totally still, without even the slightest breeze. The heat felt like a solid wall, pressing against us from all sides. We began going into the water every forty minutes, then every half-hour.

Just before we took our last dip, I saw a large gray fin slicing through the water. It was portside, perhaps thirty yards away. For a couple of seconds it veered towards us, then disappeared below the surface. Calmly, I thought: that was a shark.

I turned to Dag. "Did you just see something in the water?"

"No," he answered.

He was easing himself out of his cockpit.

"One more swim," he said. "And then we'll make a final push for Noro."

He sat on the side of the boat and, with a loud splash, fell backwards into the water. I thought: perhaps it's not a good idea.

But my body was so assaulted by heat that it wasn't interested in common sense, or in entertaining any of my usual fears and paranoias. Seconds later, I had joined Dag.

When we finally rounded a point and saw a beacon marking the opening of the harbor, we cheered. A breeze came up, so we raised our sail and cruised slowly along toward the smoking chimneys of Noro's fish processing plant. On one side of the harbor, company houses crawled up the hillside. They were ugly, dilapidated structures with plywood walls and iron roofs. On the other side, the leaf houses of a traditional village stood on stilts over the water.

After thirty hours of paddling across an empty ocean and along uninhabited jungle coastlines, we arrived at the Japanese-owned Tai-Yo factory, the place from which all the tins of tuna fish we had consumed during the past months had originated. As we came alongside a wharf, some workers ran down to greet us. They were astounded to hear that we had paddled from Vaghena; we were astounded to learn that one of them, Peter, was related to Henry.

"He's my cousin's brother," he said.

Peter took us under his wing. First, he led us to where a skipload of tuna was being hosed down with fresh water. He handed us the hose pipe, and we took turns underneath its strong gush, washing the salt out of our hair, skin and clothes. Dripping wet, we followed Peter through the factory site. After the peace and solitude of the ocean, this seemed like a bizarre dream: the clanging of skips being loaded onto cargo boats, machines pounding inside concrete buildings, radios blaring out rock music, trucks revving their engines. Japanese supervisors in pristine white shorts and shirts jumped out of brand-new jeeps and purposefully scribbled on clipboards. The heat bounced off tarmac, metal and concrete, and the still air was saturated with the smell of rancid fish.

"What time does the *Iuminau* leave?" we asked Peter, referring to the ferry, our old rat-infested friend, that was scheduled to call at Noro that night.

"The *Iuminau?*"

We nodded. "We have to get to Honiara to catch a plane."

"I take you where you can buy cold drinks!" he cried, and the subject of the *Iuminau* was dropped.

At the gates of the factory compound, Peter hailed down a passing truck and we climbed in the back. Half a mile down the road, it dropped us off at the company store. Behind the counter a heavily sweating Japanese man was in charge of the cash register, while several local teenagers ran around collecting customers' orders from the well-stocked shelves and fridges. We bought three cold beers and sat outside in the shade of a corrugated iron shelter to drink them. When we handed a can to Peter he checked that no one was watching, then hid it inside his shirt.

"If I drink this in public, I will lose my job," he explained.

"What time is the *Iuminau* coming?" Dag asked him again.

"Why don't you come to my village?" he said, pointing across the harbor. "You can stay in my house."

If it hadn't been for our alcohol-induced feelings of well-being, we might have remembered that Solomon Islanders will go to great lengths to avoid passing on bad news or giving a negative answer; we might have realized what it was Peter was trying his hardest not to tell us.

We got another lift back to the factory, where I went to use the women's washrooms. Inside, I found a girl dressed in white rubber boots, lab coat and cap, stretched out for a rest in one of the troughlike sinks. On the opposite wall were several cubicles, each with a handwritten sign stuck on the door. One read "Noro," another "Marovo," another "Munda."

"Where you from?" the girl asked.

"England," I told her. "Which toilet should I use?"

Laughing heartily, she got out of the sink, walked over to the "Noro" cubicle, ripped off the sign and ushered me inside.

When I reemerged, she was back in the sink, but sitting upright. "Where you go?" she asked.

"Honiara," I told her. "We're catching the *Iuminau* tonight." She frowned.

"*Iuminau* no coming," she said.

"It's not coming?" I repeated in alarm.

"Yesss."

"Is it coming?"

"Yesss."

I tried a new tack. "When is the *Iuminau* coming?"

She thought for a moment. "Six o'clock," she said.

Relieved, I thanked her and headed for the door. "*Iuminau* coming no more!" she called after me.

I turned back. "No?"

"Yesss," she said.

Outside, Dag was talking to a Japanese man who clutched his clipboard to his chest and bowed to me.

"I've got bad news," said Dag.

"I think I know what it is," I told him.

For reasons no one could explain to us, the *Iuminau* had sailed from Noro at six o'clock that morning, twelve hours before schedule. The next boat to Honiara wasn't due until the New Year, several days after our flight left for Australia.

In a whirl of efficiency, the Japanese man came up with solutions. There was a new road which ran through the jungle and connected Noro to the small town of Munda. At Munda there was an airstrip, and bush planes that flew to Honiara. He phoned, booked a flight, arranged for a truck. The truck came. We must hurry! he said. No time to take the boat apart now! Do it on the way to Munda! Eight burly Melanesian men lifted the fully laden boat onto their shoulders and jogged with it right through the factory compound and to the road. The truck was parked beyond a tree that had many low hanging branches. The men were heading for the tree at a steady jog.

"The mast!" cried Dag in warning. *"The maaast!"*

Too late. The aluminum pole met a low branch. The men kept jogging, their sheer strength making them unaware of the resistance. With a sickening *crack!* the central section of our mast broke in two and hit one of the men on the head. They stopped and put the boat on the ground. Catching up with them, we looked at the mast in dismay.

"Him gud no more?" asked one man.

"Problem?" inquired another.

The mast certainly was "gud no more," but there was no point worrying these kind men about it. Besides which, we were on our way to Australia, where such problems could be easily solved.

"Im gud," Dag reassured them. "No problem."

The men's faces brightened. "No problem!" they cried, and stood waving good-bye as our truck rumbled towards the jungle.

9

Hiatus in Hong Kong

"I hungry!" cried the taxi driver, stuffing his mouth with biscuits. "No time for eating, I work velly hard, but I fliddle tax man, too, ha ha!"

Trams rattled past, and above us towered Hong Kong's sheer cliff faces of glass and steel.

"OK, you tell me, where you want go really?" he asked.

"Government House," I said.

The first two taxi drivers had refused point blank to take us there. Now it seemed that this man had agreed only because he thought we were joking.

"Government House, ha! ha! You know David Wilson? Velly funny!" he chortled.

As it happened, I did know David Wilson. In 1981 I'd met him through my boyfriend, Joe Tasker, when they'd both been part of the first British mountaineering expedition to China. Joe was one of the climbers; David, who at that time was political adviser to the governor of Hong Kong, had gone along as interpreter. The last contact I'd had with David and his wife Natasha was in 1982, when they sent their condolences after Joe's death on Everest. Weeks of living in the bush must have affected my sense of propriety: during our stopover in Australia I'd faxed David, who was now governor of Hong Kong, without a second thought.

"You may not remember me . . ." I began the fax.

A reply came straight back. "Of course we remember you! Do get in touch as soon as you arrive in Hong Kong."

My sense of propriety was still amiss when from Kai Tak Airport I phoned Government House and asked to speak to David or Natasha.

"I presume," said the voice on the other end, "that you're referring to Sir and Lady Wilson."

Natasha, when she came on the line, was effusively friendly.

"Maria! We must see you! The problem is that we're awfully busy this week, and we're leaving for Bonn on Saturday, but could you come for dinner on Friday? Yes? How lovely! Where are you staying?"

"Well, we're um . . . "

A sudden wave of snobbery prevented me from admitting that we'd booked into the Hong Kong YMCA.

"We're going to find a hotel now," I lied.

"Oh, dear! We can't have you running around the city at this time of night! Look, why don't you come here? I'll have to see what I can sort out roomwise—"

"We have a tent with us— "

The words were out before I realized how stupid they were, but Natasha didn't miss a beat. "That won't be necessary, but would you mind awfully getting a taxi here? It's rather difficult to arrange for an official car at this time of night."

It wasn't until we were outside Government House, and guards had stopped the traffic in both directions to let us drive through the gates, that the taxi driver believed me.

"You really know David Wilson!" he shouted incredulously. "He a velly nice man, give him my regards, don't tell him what I said about my taxes, OK?"

Dag and I were too dumbstruck to reply. We had expected something fairly grand, but nothing like this expansive, floodlit palace. Through its porticos and down its wide steps swarmed a clutch of men in white jackets with red epaulettes. Some of them heaved our dusty baggage out of the trunk, others held open the doors of the taxi for us. As we clambered out, a uniformed official standing at the foot of the steps saluted, and a young woman ran down to greet us. She introduced herself as Elspeth the housekeeper, but she looked as if she belonged in the pages of *Tatler* magazine. As I shook her hand, I was horribly aware of my faded sulu and Dag's stained shorts and rat-chewed shirt.

"Sir David and Lady Wilson regret that they will not be able to meet you tonight," she said. "They've asked me to take you to your suite and make sure everything is comfortable for you."

Numbly, we followed her through a huge foyer, up a winding marble staircase and into the cavernous Tennis Court Suite. Sumptuously draped windows reached from the deeply carpeted floor to the high ceilings and opened onto a vast balcony. After months of sharing a small tent, we now had at our disposal two sitting rooms, two bedrooms, two bathrooms, a dressing-room, a safe and a well-stocked bar. Not to mention a servant each. Ah Hon and Janet had slipped silently into the main sitting-room, and stood waiting for us.

"If you have any laundry," said Ah Hon quietly, "we will take it now and return in the morning."

"We'll—er—have to change out of it first," I stammered.

"Could we take your order for breakfast?" asked Hon.

"Breakfast? Oh, breakfast! I really don't know—I mean I—well . . ."

"Perhaps an English breakfast, madam?" Ah Hon kindly suggested. "With grapefruit, tea, coffee?"

"Yes, of course, whatever you think . . ."

Ah Hon and Janet slid out of the room.

As soon as we were alone, I filled one of the huge baths with steaming hot water and gratefully sank into it. After the Solomon Islands and Australia, Hong Kong in January was decidedly chilly. Dag, meanwhile, headed for the bar. He brought me a gin and tonic and then wandered off clutching a glass filled with twenty-five-year-old single malt whisky. I could hear him in the bedroom, chuckling and talking to himself.

"I don't believe this! They've got to be kidding! I don't believe it!"

His voice faded away, and I sank up to my chin into the hot water. Suddenly, Dag was back.

"They're here!" he gasped.

"Who?"

"The Wilsons! There was a knock on the door, I thought it was Ah Hon or Janet, and in they walked, and me with these filthy clothes and a bucketful of whisky in my hand! Come on, they're waiting to see you!"

He grabbed one of the long, fluffy bathrobes hanging on the wall, and thrust it at me. I had a brief glance at myself in the dressing-room mirror as I hurried out, and saw tousled, wet hair framing a lobster-like face.

As the Wilsons greeted me with hugs and kisses I held my breath, fearful of overpowering them with gin fumes. They were exactly as I remembered them: David tall and distinguished, with sharp yet kindly features; and Natasha with black hair framing a pale complexion and a ready smile.

"We're on our way out, but we thought we'd pop by first to say hello," said Natasha.

They perched on chair arms, quite relaxed, while Dag stood shifting uncomfortably from one foot to the other. Amid the luxurious furnishing of the sitting-room, and next to David and Natasha, who were suitably dressed for the function they were about to attend, he looked impossibly disheveled.

"One of our sons sometimes turns up from his travels looking just like you," Natasha reassured him. "We find it rather refreshing."

The starched linen sheets we slept between had crown insignia embroidered on them, and when I woke up thirsty during the night, I reached for the silver flask next to my bed and poured water from it into a crystal glass. At 7:30 we heard faint clinking sounds from the sitting-room. I opened the adjoining door a crack and peeked in. A table had been brought into the room and was being laid by Ah Hon and Janet, who were moving around as if on wheels. On the dot of 8:00 we were summoned for breakfast. The table was set with fine china and silver. The eggs were perfectly cooked, the tea piping hot, and there were newspapers from Hong Kong, Britain and America.

After breakfast, Ah Hon and Janet slipped past us to deliver two pathetically small piles of laundry to our bedroom. In what was nothing short of a miracle, someone had removed most of the stains from Dag's shorts and rat-chewed shirt, and then meticulously ironed the tattered garments. My faded sulu, T-shirt and underwear had been similarly treated.

"Do have any laundry for this morning?" asked Janet.

"Well—er—no, not yet, we'll have to change out of it . . ."

Despite our scruffy appearance, everyone in Government House made us feel at home. Elsewhere, however, we were subjected to puzzled scrutiny.

"Where are you staying in Hong Kong?" asked the bank clerk

who was filling in a form to arrange a cash advance on our credit card. When we told him, his pen froze in midair and he gave us a long, withering look before writing "In Transit" on the form. A similar incredulity met us at the British Airways office, where we went to broach the subject of excess baggage on our forthcoming flight to New Delhi. The official who phoned me to further discuss the matter was stunned into silence to find that the unsophisticated creature she'd met the previous day was, in fact, a guest of the governor.

For two days we rushed around Hong Kong, dazzled by its pace and its mind-boggling contrasts. After a morning spent sorting out our affairs in the business district, where immaculately dressed men and women bustled along talking into cellular phones, we turned a corner and found ourselves outside the Central Market. A dank stairwell led up to a first floor which was wall to wall with chickens. There were live chickens crammed into bamboo cages and stacked eight high, dead chickens hanging in rows from meat hooks, dismembered chickens arranged on stone counters into neat piles of livers, hearts, wings, heads and feet. Incongruous among them all was one lonely heron, magnificently feathered, hunched up and peering with beady eyes through the bars of its cage.

"Will you eat him?" I hesitantly asked a woman who was washing a chicken carcass in a vat of bloody water. She promptly dropped the bird, which sank from sight, grabbed a cleaver and headed for the heron. Hurriedly, we sorted out the misunderstanding and escaped to the vegetable market on the floor above.

In the evenings we sought out alleyway Chinese restaurants, tiny places where no one spoke English and we rarely knew what we were ordering. But on Friday night we had dinner with the Wilsons in a blue and white room hung with signed portraits of visiting royals. Servants hovered at a discreet distance, watching carefully to ascertain when they were needed. Each time they came to set down a plate or pick up a glass, Natasha thanked them by name. I was impressed by her faultless courtesy, and told her so.

"Oh, I couldn't be any other way, the staff here are wonderful, they're like family. We shall miss them dreadfully."

David, who was casually dressed in white pants, a red sweater and bright red socks, had a preoccupied air. Two weeks before, he had been informed by the British prime minister that he was to retire after just over five years, and that a new governor would oversee Hong Kong's transition from British sovereignty to Chinese control. Despite this, he found time to be worried about us and the way we were haphazardly lurching around the world.

"How are you getting your kayak to India?" he asked. "Isn't it costing a fortune to fly it there?"

"British Airways has agreed to waive excess baggage charges," I told him.

His eyebrows rose. "Well done. They're usually pretty sticky about that sort of thing. How did you manage it?"

A blush spread upwards from my neck. "I—sort of—well—mentioned—ah—that I was staying here."

"How enterprising of you," he said, and the conversation switched to the Peking Duck we were eating.

Our flight to New Delhi left the following evening, and the Wilsons insisted that first we should go on a tour around some of the beauty spots of the New Territories. At noon, our driver Raymond held open the doors of a shiny black limousine which had gold crown insignia instead of number plates. We slid through the streets of the city, and when we stopped at traffic lights curious pedestrians gathered to peer at the two unlikely characters inside one of the Governor's cars. We were beyond the city limits and on our way to Lion Rock Park when I leaned back and said, "Funny to think that tonight we'll be in New Delhi."

"No kidding," said Dag. "How come we don't need visas for India?"

My stomach lurched, then went into a tight knot. Arranging visas for India had been my job, one I was supposed to do in Australia. One I had totally forgotten about.

There was a phone in the back seat. I called Elspeth and asked her for advice.

"All the consulates are closed now," she told me, "but I'll track down the private numbers of consulate staff and get back to you."

"Please," I said, "don't tell Sir David and Lady Wilson about this."

"I wouldn't dream of it."

While Raymond cruised us around Lion Rock Park, I gabbled down the phone to a series of Indian officials. They told me that visas took between one and four weeks to come through, and that I should have thought about them sooner. Abject apologies, self-recrimination and some furious name-dropping seemed to soften the rules. By the time the limousine slid to the main entrance of Government House, I'd arranged for a meeting with a high-ranking official of the Indian consulate early on Monday morning. I'd also rescheduled our flights to Monday night and booked a room at the YMCA. As if he hadn't heard a word of the conversations on the back seat, Raymond turned and said, "I will be collecting you at seven to take you to the airport."

"We won't be going there, we'll be going to—" began Dag, but I silenced him with a sharp poke in the ribs.

"We can't turn up at the YMCA in a Government House limousine," I hissed.

"Why not? God, you and your inverted snobbery," he said, and leaned forward to Raymond.

"You'll be taking us to the YMCA instead," he told him.

Once again, I was in the bathroom when David and Natasha called into our suite. They were on their way to Bonn, and they wanted to say good-bye. By the time I emerged Dag had already spilled the beans and Natasha was sitting on a chair arm next to our heap of baggage, wringing her hands.

"Oh Maria, I'm so sorry, how absolutely dreadful for you to spend all afternoon worrying. You should have let us know, I'm sure we could have helped."

"It's all my fault anyway," I explained. "A stupid mistake, I just forgot—"

"But that's so easy to do! It happens to all of us!"

"You did awfully well, arranging a visa for Monday," said David, looking a trifle uneasy. "How did you manage it?"

Natasha suppressed a smile as I blundered through an explanation.

"I mean, I didn't use your name exactly," I said eventually, "but I sort of mentioned that we were staying here."

"Well done," he said.

"Now about this idea of yours to move to a hotel," said Natasha.

I gave Dag a grateful glance. "You've been so kind already and really it's no trouble for us to—"

"We won't hear of it!" she cried. "You must stay here until Monday. We'll be gone and there will only be a skeleton staff, but I'm sure Ah Hon and Janet will come in to make your breakfast and see to your laundry."

Monday was Dag's birthday, and I gave him a small brass monkey with lucky coins on its back, a little talisman I'd picked up the day before on one of the stalls along Ladder Street. As this was the Year of the Monkey, his sign in the Chinese horoscope, it seemed an apt gift.

"I hope it brings us luck today," he said.

The Indian Consulate was in the business sector of the city, a brave new world of glass-covered walkways that spanned roads and connected high-rises. On the sixteenth floor of the United Center, we were ushered into the high-ranking official's office. From behind his vast polished desk, he slowly looked us up and down.

"Let us sit together on the sofa," he said, gesturing towards acres of upholstered leather. "May I offer you coffee?"

A button was pressed, coffee was brought and poured from a silver pot. I tried to stop my hand from trembling as I lifted the cup to my lips. The high-ranking official, by contrast, was supremely composed.

"How unfortunate that you have no visas. How did this come to be?"

I decided on honesty. "It's my fault. I simply forgot. I know this is terribly inconvenient, but we are on a tight schedule and it's very important for us to get to India by tonight."

Turning one of his gold cuff links, he considered this for a few seconds. My coffee cup rattled as I set it down on the saucer.

"I believe you are guests of the governor? How very nice. What is the purpose of your visit to India?"

"We're going to kayak down the Ganges," I told him, adding what I thought might be helpful information, "and collect material for a book."

"So you are writers?"

"Yes."

"No," said Dag, pressing his foot hard against mine.

"That's right," I said. "Not really, I mean it was only an idea, there's nothing arranged, we don't have a contract or anything—"

As the pressure of Dag's foot increased, I realized it was time to shut up.

"It is possible for us, in special circumstances, to arrange tourist visas at short notice," said the high-ranking official. "But visas for the purpose of business are a very different matter. A very different matter indeed. And far more expensive. Perhaps I should pose the question once more. What is the purpose of your visit to India?"

"A holiday," answered Dag.

"Absolutely," I added.

The high-ranking official gave us the ghost of a smile. "Very good. Your visas will be ready by four o'clock."

The plane banked steeply; below us, the anchor lights of hundreds of boats hovered like fireflies in the harbor, and along neon-red roads cutting through the forest of glittering high-rises, car head lamps streamed and flashed and searched. A cloud engulfed us; Hong Kong, with all its glamour and excitement, was suddenly gone. We sat back and began to nervously consider the next part of our journey.

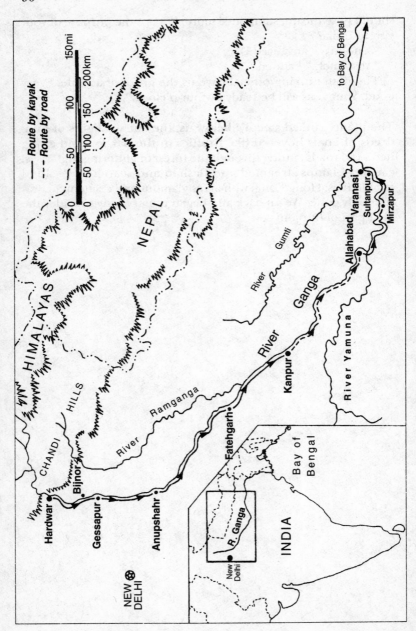

10

A Holy River

"Kayaking along the Ganges!" cried Mr. Gupta, a government official in New Delhi. "You must be potty!"

Long before we arrived in India, Dag and I had become inured to such comments. They had followed us from Canada halfway across the world in letters, in phone calls, in chance conversations. We'd been urged to drop our plan and opt for something safer and more sanitary. Once we were in India, however, we had hoped to find some encouragement: after all, Hindus believe that the river embodies the Goddess Ganga, that its waters have the power of physical and spiritual purification and of releasing a soul from the painful cycle of rebirth. If only a little of the river's holiness rubbed off on us along the way, surely we'd be all right? Mr. Gupta didn't think so.

"I am a devout Hindu," he said, "but when it comes to bathing in the Ganges I struggle between my faith and my knowledge of bacteriology. I beg you to reconsider this journey."

At two minutes past midnight on a January night, we'd dragged our baggage past sleepy customs and passport control officials and out into the forecourt of New Delhi Airport. The air was cool, and so polluted with exhaust fumes, grit and smoke that it stung the backs of our throats. A taxi driver wearing a lumpy hand-knitted sweater and an old tweed jacket led us to his Hindustani Ambassador, a copy of the British 1950s Morris Oxford. He carefully steered the vehicle around a cow that sat ruminating in the airport driveway, then barreled along a wide boulevard beneath dim yellowish streetlights. Apart from a few scooters, there was little other traffic about. On either side of the boulevard, old trees grew behind high stone walls, suggesting the unseen presence of imposing residences. In front of them were stalls covered with tarpaulins, huddles of shacks, and men sleeping on handcarts.

"Welcome to the Maurya Sheraton," said a smiling young woman attired in a gorgeous green and gold silk sari. "We are greatly pleased to be hosting you."

From Canada I had contacted the Maurya Sheraton, one of New Delhi's most exclusive hotels, suggesting that in return for hospitality we could offer some useful promotion. It seemed like a long shot, but a positive and enthusiastic reply had come by return of post.

"The yacht, Government House and now this," muttered Dag, as a gold-mirrored lift smoothly whisked us up to the deeply carpeted Executive Suite. "And I thought we were supposed to be the adventurous types!"

"We'll be sleeping in the mud soon enough," I assured him.

Early next morning, we gazed over a scene made silent by the triple-glazed windows of our room. A large brown garuda bird flapped by like some prehistoric creature. On the boulevard, traffic was snarled up by a train of fifty camels ridden by straight-backed soldiers. Beyond it, miles of parkland stretched away, and the only sign of the city was a dense gray-blue haze that hung over the treetops.

A concierge in red livery and turban saluted us and held the door open as we left the hotel. The morning was warm and muggy. Waiting at the end of the hotel driveway was a line of autorickshaws, yellow and black vehicles that were little more than three-wheeled scooters with double passenger seats and canopies. Their drivers leaned against them, smoking small, pungent cigarettes called *bidis.*

"Where to, sir?" cried one.

"Connaught Place."

"I have no knowledge of this place, sir."

Connaught Place, which we tried pronouncing in every conceivable way, is the commercial heart of New Delhi. Yet none of the drivers who had gathered around to listen to our verbal acrobatics appeared to have heard of it. An elderly man walking out of the hotel grounds stopped to see what was going on. He carried a briefcase and wore a sports jacket and a *dhoti*, fifteen feet of cotton tied around his waist and looped between his legs.

"May I be of assistance to you?" he asked. We explained our dilemma.

"Connaught Place!" he told the autorickshaw driver, who immediately understood him. "And don't charge an anna more than twenty-five rupees!"

It was rather like some terrifying fairground ride, where you pay to be scared witless. Traffic rules, if any existed, were ignored, especially on the large roundabouts, where cars cut across us with inches to spare, buses loomed up and veered away, and we swerved around scooters on which women rode side-saddle, their shawls and saris fluttering behind them like flags. There was a cacophony of ringing bells, honking horns and squealing brakes, and vivid images flashed by: men lathered themselves at standpipes or sat on wooden chairs having their faces shaved, their heads massaged, their nose and ear hairs clipped. Shutters banged open to reveal the interiors of bike repair shops, shops selling ropes and brass pots, shops filled with baskets of roses and marigolds. At a construction site, women in saris and heavy pewter anklets carried piles of bricks on their heads. Cows, pigs and goats foraged amid rubbish swept into piles at the side of the road. School children with satchels slung over immaculate uniforms picked their way around the rubbish and the dung. At traffic lights, beneath a sign exhorting drivers to PLEASE STOP WHEN LIGHT IS RED, we came to a halt. Beggars ran up and extended skinny arms and upturned palms into the autorickshaw. Around them, pale sunlight shafted through dusty air, air which smelled of exhaust fumes, flowers, roasting peanuts and urine.

In Connaught Place roads radiated from a bustling circle like wheel spokes, and torrents of cars, autorickshaws and scooters poured along them, horns honking and bells ringing, hell bent, it seemed, on exterminating pedestrians.

"Fifty-five rupees, please sir," shouted the driver.

"That gentleman at the hotel said you should charge no more than twenty-five."

"*Fifty*-five rupees the gentleman was saying, *fifty*-five!"

Grateful to have survived the ride, we couldn't be bothered to argue. And now, to get to Mr. Gupta's office, we had to cross the road. As we stood up on the curb, plucking up enough courage to face the onslaught of traffic and merciless drivers, it occurred to me that gathering information on the Ganges could be far more dangerous than paddling along it.

Our plan was to transport the kayak to Hardwar, where the Ganges leaves the Himalayas and enters the great northern plains. From there we hoped to paddle to the holy city of Varanasi, thus traveling along the most revered part of the river, and across the huge state of Uttar Pradesh. In search of maps and pertinent information, we climbed one dank stairwell after another and sat in the gloomy offices of government officials amid desks and shelves piled high with tattered papers. The dark-suited men we met told us how much wastewater gets pumped each day into the Ganges, or Ganga as it is more commonly known in India, and how many sewage plants and electric crematoria are being built along its banks. They also warned us of its bandits and the unsanitary living conditions of its villages. But they couldn't provide us with a detailed map of the river, or advise of its premonsoon water levels, or even agree on the distance by river between Hardwar and Varanasi.

"It's six hundred and fifty miles," said Colonel Kumar, of the Indian Mountaineering Association.

Having given up on government officials, we were now exploring other channels of information. We met with the colonel in the Gymkhana Club, a crumbling monument to bygone colonial days, where we sat on vinyl-covered sofas beneath high, arched ceilings, while waiters pushed trolleys over creaking wooden floors and served us with china cups of lukewarm tea.

"Don't worry about maps!" Colonel Kumar assured us. "You won't be needing them."

Some years before he had stage-managed Sir Edmund Hillary's expedition by high-powered speedboat up the Ganga, and he seemed to have similar ideas for us.

"For twenty thousand rupees I can provide for three weeks a land support crew of jeep, driver and guide," he told us. "This crew will meet you each day at prearranged spots along the river, set up your camp, cordon it off to keep away the locals, and cook for you."

We explained that our idea was to meander along the Ganges as whim and fortune took us, and to learn about local life without having to worry unduly about schedules or time pressures. Singularly unimpressed by this, the colonel quickly lost interest in us and advised us to contact a Mr. Koli, who ran the Wild Life Adventure Tours.

"I estimate the distance you will have to travel is at least nine hundred and fifty miles," said Avinash Koli, sensibly adding, "but Mother Ganga is flooding her banks and changing her course every year, so really she is the one you should ask."

Unlike most people we'd met in New Delhi, he regarded our plan with open enthusiasm.

"The journey will spiritually uplift you," he promised. "And it will be a great adventure—I know of no one who has kayaked on this part of the Ganga. But you will have problems with bandits, and the people there speak only Hindi. You must take a guide. I will send you my best man. He is an experienced kayaker and his English is faultless."

Silently, I wondered how we could be guided along a river which no one had kayaked on before. But after our few days in India we'd already grown used to such illogicalities; we struck a deal with Koli and arranged to meet up with his man in Hardwar.

In Old Delhi Bus Station, stunned by the hubbub of whistles, shouts, revving engines, honking horns and shrill, incomprehensible announcements, we watched two porters hoist our red bags onto their heads and promptly disappear behind a muddle of buses. It took half an hour of frantic chasing about before we relocated the bags, which were in fact strapped on to the roof of the Hardwar bus. The 120-mile journey took ten bone-rattling hours and included innumerable stops at squalid towns along the way. The bus was packed: between our second-row seat and the driver's cabin I counted seventeen adults, four children, six sacks, three bedrolls, four suitcases and eight boxes. A baby in the seat in front of us threw up every half-hour or so; each time he erupted his mother cupped her hand to catch the vomit, and smeared it on the side of the bus. We arrived in Hardwar after dark, amid a blustery rainstorm. The bus station was on a narrow street of shuttered and heavily padlocked shopfronts. A large billboard advertised "Orbit TV—The Divine Choice." A few scrawny cows loafed about, and a man who had just finished defecating in the gutter squatted by a puddle to wash himself.

The Tourist Bungalow was cold and bleak, and we were the

only guests in its restaurant. Our waiter was bundled up in an old jacket and a thick woolen scarf, and the index finger of his right hand was wrapped in a thick wad of dirty bandage. Before setting our plates down before us, he breathed hard on them and wiped them with a gray rag. The meal, however, was delicious: flat, pan-fried bread called *roti*, and *paneer bhuji*, a delicious mixture of scrambled milk curds and chopped vegetables. We ate quickly, then went to our room. In the adjoining latrine I had a strip wash in a bucket of lukewarm water, and tried to banish from my mind thoughts of the Maurya Sheraton's luxurious bathrooms. Dag was already fast asleep when I joined him beneath the heavy cotton quilt. All night, a cold wind blew down from the Himalayan foothills and whistled through the broken window and under the ill-fitting door of our room.

Koli's "best man," Bapi Sakar, had already arrived from New Delhi by deluxe bus, and we met him in the guest house over a breakfast of milk porridge and *chapatis*. A Bengali in his early twenties, he was small and wiry, with a dazzling smile and mop of black curls. Dressed in an oversized woolen sweater, baggy knee-length shorts and baseball boots, he looked like an Indian caricature of an American teenager, and he exuded a self-confidence to match.

"I've done a Wilderness Survival Course," he told us, reeling off an unrequested curriculum vitae. "I can catch fish and turtles and make a shelter in the woods. I've studied under India's most famous ornithologist, I've guided whitewater kayak tours in Canada and the States, I've led treks in the Garwal Himalayas, I can identify flowers and wildlife, and once an elephant charged me and I was almost killed!"

He had with him a map of Uttar Pradesh, a plastic whitewater kayak without a rudder, a leaky tent and an ample supply of bidis. But he had no food, stove or cooking equipment. His first job, we decided, would be to guide us to Hardwar market and help us buy provisions for the trip along the Ganga.

From an open-fronted grocery where goods were displayed in sacks on the wooden floor and weighed out on brass scales, we bought rice, lentils, milk powder, biscuits, tea and sugar. From a murky back room with grease-smeared walls we bought ghee, or clarified butter. From vendors who couldn't understand why foreign tourists should want such things, we bought a kerosene lamp, paraffin and rough woolen blankets for the cold nights.

And from a canopied road stall we bought onions, carrots, ginger and garlic. The stall was hemmed in between a wall and a tight knot of people, scooters and cows. While we were stuffing the vegetables into our bags, a funeral procession came by. A body covered by a thin white sheet and strewn with marigolds was carried on a rough stretcher by eight men. They weaved their way through the crowd, and to get past the dense section where we stood, they lifted the stretcher above their heads. The body shifted, and for one horrible moment I thought it was about to tumble off and land on our shoulders.

The river below Hardwar was in an alarmingly shrunken state, as much of it had been diverted into the Upper Ganges Canal, and the rest was at its premonsoon level. We assembled our kayak on some steps, or *ghats,* leading down to a narrow channel of gray-green water. Opposite us was a row of temples and ashrams; ahead, the flood plain rolled away, dry and dusty, towards the Chandi Hills. A little way downstream, a line of *dhobi wallahs*— laundry men—were standing ankle deep in the river, ferociously beating rocks with articles of clothing.

"Swack! Hah! Swack! Hah! Swack! Hah!"

The men whipped the garments into the air and brought them down hard—Swack!—on the rock, with an accompanying shout of "Hah!" Our arrival gave the clothes a temporary reprieve, because as soon as we started to assemble our boat, the dhobi wallahs abandoned their work and crowded around us.

Half an hour later, our kayak had begun to take shape. I was on my haunches, fitting a plastic combing around the back cockpit, while Dag, with his head, shoulders and arms inside the front cockpit, was struggling with a piece of the aluminum frame. The laundry men had been joined by some friends; knees pressed against my back as I crouched over the kayak, eyes stared into mine from inches away, and I suddenly realized that I couldn't see the bag containing the rest of our gear—our camping equipment, stove, food and clothes. All the warnings we'd received about theft along the Ganges had convinced us that if we didn't constantly keep an eye on our belongings we'd be left with only the clothes on our backs. I struggled to my feet, the men stepped back to form a corridor for me, and there was the bag, lying undisturbed behind them. I dragged it forward and sat on it, and the men rearranged themselves around me. One of them, a hollow-cheeked old man with enormous ears, leaned forward.

"What is the nature of your business here?" he shouted.

"We will travel in this boat to Varanasi," I told him.

When the old man translated this news for our audience, there was a murmur of approval. "A *yatra*, madam," he said. "A pilgrimage."

"No—"

"Excuse me, madam, but yes. You are traveling from one holy place to another along Mother Ganga. This is a pilgrimage, and it will purify you of all sin."

According to Hindu lore, any journey along the Ganges must begin with a *puja*, or act of worship, and I was far too superstitious to eschew this tradition. From one of the temples, Bapi summoned a *pujari*, a Hindu priest, who arrived holding a stainless steel tray heaped with marigolds, a coconut, banana leaves and an assortment of small brass pots. When the kayaks were ready and packed we climbed into them, and the pujari crouched down next to us. After wedging burning incense sticks between the stone slabs of the ghats, he rang a small bell and the puja began. Murmuring prayers, he tied red strings to our wrists and kayaks, and smudged our foreheads with *tikkas* of sandalwood paste. I lowered onto the river an offering of a tiny banana-leaf boat filled with marigolds, sweets and burning camphor. A coconut was cracked open and its milk sprinkled over us and the kayaks. The flesh was broken into pieces and passed around; eagerly the dhobi wallahs reached for this *prasad*, or blessed food, and touched it to their foreheads before eating it. Finally, the pujari bade us drink three times from the river. With deep misgivings about the effect of Ganges water on my system, I scooped some up in my palm and took a tentative sip.

"You must drink three times!" Bapi reminded me. The puja completed, I placed 100 rupees onto the tray.

"Give one more," whispered Bapi. "Even numbers are unlucky."

The pujari took the money in his right palm, counted it, then lifted it to his forehead.

"Ganga ma kijai!" yelled Bapi. "We salute you, Mother Ganga!"

The watching crowd took up the cry—"Ganga ma kijai!"—but their words were whipped away by the wind and lost somewhere in the vast expanse of sky and space that lay ahead of us.

11

Arduous Days

Although our kayak floats in a few inches of water, it got barely 200 yards down the Ganga before running aground on a gravel shoal. As we pushed the boat free, we cracked jokes about being stuck so soon after embarking on so long a journey. Four hours and fifteen gravel shoals later, the jokes had worn thin. The channel was winding languidly across the plain and dividing up into a tangled skein of shallow waterways. By the time we stopped for the day, we estimated that after paddling a total of eight miles we were a mile and a half from where we'd started. We had six weeks to reach Varanasi. If, as Mr. Koli had insisted, it was 950 miles away, to get there we would have to achieve a daily average of twenty-three miles—which meant that already we were behind schedule.

"We'll never make it," I whined as we unpacked the kayak.

"Don't worry!" said Dag, as sanguine as ever. "Things can only get better!"

Considering how disheartened I felt, it's fortunate that I had no idea of how wrong he was.

We camped that first night on a large arrow-shaped sand island that stood high between two channels. For safety's sake, we erected the tents facing each other, with the kayaks between them. Crows and mynah birds hopped about the patches of scrubby grass, doubtless surprised to see humans on this desolate and transitory scrap of land. I was on my way down the bank to fill our kettle when I saw two strange creatures silently sliding across the surface of the water. They appeared to have misshapen heads and truncated torsos, and it was only as my eyes adjusted to the fading light, and as the creatures drew closer, that I recognized them as men. Wrapped in shawls, they were sitting on bamboo slats laid across inflated inner tubes which they propelled with small, spoon-shaped wooden paddles. I stared wonderingly at them; they stared wonderingly back. Dag and Bapi appeared beside me, and Bapi began talking to the men in an exchange so shrill and high pitched that it sounded argumentative. As I soon came to recognize, this was the tone of almost every conversation in Hindi, however mild and uncontroversial the subject being discussed.

"They are fishermen," Bapi told us. "They are coming to put down their nets. They are saying that there are *dacoits* around here, that it is not safe for us to camp alone. They are wanting us to go with them to their village of Agitpur." The thought of dacoits was unappealing, but so was the prospect of taking down the tents, packing up the boats, paddling across the river, unpacking the boats and hauling them for over a kilometer. We decided to stay put and take our chances. The men set their nets, turned and silently slid across the surface of the river, disappearing into the deepening gloom. The sun slipped away, leaving an eerie orange glow and a sickle moon in its wake. While I made notes by the kerosene lamp, Dag and Bapi fired up our tiny stove and cooked *kedgeree*, a mess of rice and curried vegetables. From somewhere beyond our small circle of light, a jackal began to bark and laugh. Another joined in, then several more, and soon the air was filled by the mad frenzy of their calls.

At first light, we were woken by the sound of revving engines. The rocks and gravel we had cursed the afternoon before were obviously valued here: men were throwing boulders into the back of the trucks and sieving gravel through baskets woven from branches. With dismay, we watched a fully laden truck ford the river downstream of our campsite, the water barely covering the bottom of its tires.

"I never expected to get run over on the Ganges," sighed Dag.

Beyond the trucks, a herd of wild blue buffalo ambled along, touched by the glow of the rising sun. Away on the horizon, mist rose from the blur of trees marking the far side of the flood plain, the Chandi Hills were softly etched against the sky and a glistening snow-capped mountain peeped above them.

As I dipped our tea kettle into the river, the remnant of a marigold garland twirled by in an eddy and caught in the spout. Carried downstream from Hardwar, the debris of pujas was strewn all along the banks: flowers and coconuts and scraps of red cloth. Doubtfully, I peered into the brimming kettle. The water was gray and thick with sediment. I emptied it out, waded into the river and refilled the kettle from a faster current. I was about to turn back to the shore when I noticed three men on the opposite bank. They were hunkered down, completely covered by blankets and as motionless as statues. They were still there an hour later when, after a quick breakfast of tea and biscuits, I was back at the water's edge with my toothbrush and toothpaste. I had rather hoped to get around cleaning my teeth in the river, but our ceramic filter was struggling with the amount of silt it had to deal with, and was only producing enough water for drinking purposes. I gave my teeth a cursory scrub and spat out as much of the river water as I possibly could. The statues gazed at me, unnerving in their stillness. When we paddled off, their heads very slowly turned to watch our progress downstream.

Although the river was soon boosted by a couple of tributaries, it continued to spread out and subdivide. Each time it branched we had to make a decision about which channel to take. Sometimes, choosing wrong, we paddled into dead ends and had to haul the boats across gravel banks back to the main channel. This was exhausting work, but at least we had a remarkable array of birds to distract us. There were sandpipers, egrets, cranes, mergansers, eagles, kingfishers and many more we couldn't identify.

"What's that bird, Bapi?" I once asked him.

"Which bird?"

"There—it's black with a white belly and an iridescent green neck."

There was a long silence, a sign that I was soon to realize meant he didn't know the answer to a question, so was busily making one up.

"It's called a Black Indian Bastard!" he finally pronounced.

Twice, while we were hauling the boat, I slipped on the smooth stones and managed to get thoroughly wet in three inches of water. I flung imprecations at the gravel banks, but by midafternoon I was longing for their return. The river seemed to be progressively wearing down the land it traveled over. Boulders became rocks, rocks became gravel, gravel became sand and the sand itself was sifted down to a state so fine that, although well nigh invisible, it could be borne on the breeze and deposited in our ears, noses and eyes. And worse, it could mingle with water to form nightmarish traps.

The sandbank that snared us was concealed just below the surface of the turbid water. With resigned sighs, Dag and I climbed out of the kayak to push it free. Something sucked at my feet, cold mud closed around my ankles and I realized I was sinking into the riverbed.

"Quicksand!" cried Dag.

Before either of us had time to react we were up to our knees in the evil stuff. We threw ourselves over the cockpits, hauled ourselves free and awkwardly tumbled back into our seats.

Eight more patches of quicksand awaited us. By the end of our second day on the river, we and the inside of the kayak were smeared with a layer of Ganges mud.

The river swung away from the Chandi Hills, the plain widened to nine miles across and the horizon became as flat as if we were at sea. We were traveling through one of the most densely populated parts of India, along a river that was a lifeline to millions, yet there was no one and nothing in sight, only an arching, empty sky and an immense expanse of silver-gray desert. As we wormed our way across it, I sometimes imagined how we must have looked from high above. I fancied someone peering down from a plane and picking out two tiny dots, one red and one blue, unrecognizable as boats. It was a humbling thought. During those arduous days, I felt myself shrinking away in the midst of this solitary wasteland until I was a mere speck, almost swallowed up by space, light and silence.

Each night's campsite was more desolate than the last. There was a day of rain, when the sand flats were transmuted to a muddy moonscape and honking geese flew furiously above us as if heading to a warmer place. Cold, damp and miserable, I kept asking myself why we'd come here and how we'd survive weeks of this numbing desolation.

And then, after days of nothingness, people appeared. Standing on the white sand, etched against the empty sky, men swathed in brown blankets with mattocks slung over their shoulders, women in bright cotton saris carrying shiny brass bowls on their heads. With them, a buffalo pulling a wooden wheeled cart. This was time rolled back, a scene unchanged for hundreds of years. At first, the people were rendered mute with astonishment at the sight of us. But when we pressed our palms together and called out greetings they rushed down the bank and bombarded Bapi with questions about where we'd come from, where we were going.

"Hardwar sey, Varanasi tak? Yatra!" "Hardwar to Varanasi? A pilgrimage!"

They told us they were walking to their fields from their village, and pointed back across the empty plain.

"How much longer must you walk?" we asked them.

"Two hours," they replied, "maybe three, maybe four."

There was the same vagueness when we asked about distances.

"How far to the Bijnor barrage?"

"Thirty-five kilometers," they said.

The next people we met told us it was fifty kilometers away, the next said seventy-five. As Bapi had left the map of Uttar Pradesh in his hotel room in Hardwar, he was trying to navigate with our map of the subcontinent of India, constantly poring over it, measuring distances with string and coming up with estimates as wildly varying as the ones the farmers were giving us.

On our fourth day we rounded a bend in the river and saw the outline of the Bijnor Barrage a kilometer or so away. Pulling into a back eddy, we waited for Bapi to catch up with us. On the bank, a dead cow was being picked over by some enormous brown-black vultures which hopped around in an ungainly way, sticking their heads and hideous necks right inside the cow's gaping chest cavity. A little farther along some men were reinforcing a section of the riverbank, piling up bags of stone behind a retaining wall built of branches, which looked as if it would be whisked away by the first hint of the monsoon. The men waved at us, shouting and pointing toward the barrage.

"They are saying we can paddle through the barrage," said Bapi, when he arrived.

"Through the barrage?"

"They are saying a channel is there and we can follow it."

"Yes, and it probably drops fifty feet on the other side of the barrage."

He thought for a moment. "Perhaps it is nonsense for us to be going to the trouble of a portage when we could be paddling through the barrage."

Bapi was overruled, and we pulled out of the river a hundred yards away from the barrage. It was a huge structure of concrete and blue metal that doubled as a road bridge. From the girders, black-faced monkeys swung above the trucks that rumbled to and from the nearby town of Bijnor. At river level, only one of the barrage's iron gates was open; a torrent of water funneled through it and became a crashing waterfall on the other side.

While we began to unpack our kayak, Bapi went to hire some men as porters. After half an hour he returned with a father and son. The father was old, half blind and wafer thin, while his son had a heavily bandaged left hand and a vacant expression on his face.

"They want twenty-five rupees each," said Bapi.

By our standards this was a pittance, the equivalent of a dollar each, but by theirs it was a handsome fee, a day's wages for carrying some heavy bags for 200 yards. Bapi relayed to them our acceptance of this price, but by now they were staring intently at the boats and bags. The old man looked up at Dag and served him a volley of rapid Hindi.

"He is saying," Bapi translated, "that this is too much for them. He is saying that for one hundred rupees extra they will walk back to their village and bring a bullock cart here."

"And how long will that take?" asked Dag. "It's not far across the barrage. Tell them we'll all help with the portage."

Bapi looked alarmed. "Really, I am thinking that the bullock cart is a good idea. And anyway, they are insisting on it."

"Tell them we'll find someone else," said Dag.

This incensed the porters, who claimed we could not break the verbal contract we'd made with them. We countered by saying that the contract had not included a bullock cart. There was a lengthy discussion, involving much head-waggling and repetitions of "Acchha," which can mean, according to context, "OK" or "I see" or "oh, really?" or "very good." Finally, a compromise was reached and a plan agreed upon. Dag, Bapi and the porters would carry as much gear as they could across the bridge while I stayed to guard the rest. Then Bapi would remain on the far side of the bridge while Dag and the porters returned for a second carry.

It didn't work out like that. We divided the contents of our kayak between the two red sacks. Dag lifted one sack onto his shoulder and set off across the bridge, the porters carried the kayak behind him, I sat on the other sack and Bapi started to unpack his boat. He was still unpacking it when the two porters sauntered back. I stood up and pointed to the sack. The old man shook his head and shot off down the embankment towards Bapi. The younger man picked up the sack, staggered a few steps, dropped it in the middle of the road and went to join his father. Ten minutes later they reappeared, one carrying Bapi's light plastic boat and the other his bags, while Bapi walked behind them, empty-handed and with a regal air.

"You'll have to help me with this bag," I hissed at him, in a tone so icy he obviously thought better of demurring.

A half-hour's paddle from the barrage, we camped in the shade of a grassy sand dune. A farmer was there, preparing a field to plant pumpkins and watermelons. He was heaping sand into long mounds to demarcate the field, sticking sheaves of dried grass into the mounds to act as windbreaks, digging hollows and filling them with soil and seedlings he'd brought by bullock cart from his village. Each day, he said, he would return here to water the crop, which he would harvest before the monsoon, when his painstakingly created field would disappear beneath the river. And for this he would receive fifty paise—half a rupee for each kilo of watermelons and pumpkins, which would then be sold in the market for ten rupees a kilo. Why, I asked, didn't he sell the produce himself?

"I am not of the market seller caste," he answered.

Bathed in evening light, the sand was golden, the sky a delicate blue and the grasses a soft yellow. Geese wandered up and down the shoreline, and as darkness fell their honking mingled with the barking of jackals and the hum of distant traffic. The lights of the barrage were faulty, and throughout the night they blinked on and off in an unintentional and disconcerting *son et lumière*. Around 2 A.M. I crawled out of the tent to pee. The lights snapped on and illuminated two figures paddling on inner tubes across the river towards our campsite. I shook Dag awake, but by the time he'd poked his head out of the tent door the lights were off.

"I can't see anyone," he said.

The lights snapped on again, outlining the two figures about to reach the shore, not twenty yards away.

"*Hey! You!*" Dag shouted. "What do you think you're up to?"

The figures froze. The barrage lights snapped off. When they came on again two minutes later, the inner tube people were heading back across the river in the direction from which they'd come.

We slept fitfully, and at 5:30 decided we might as well get up. The river was shrouded in a cold mist which swallowed up the blinking lights of the barrage and intensified the sense of desolation. The quick wash I had in the river froze me to the core, and I piled on every article of clothing I had and paddled off with my teeth chattering. We hadn't gone far before we saw a human skull amid the dry yellow grass on the bank. A little farther along, a full skeleton lay on its back with its knees askew. The river continued to wind and divide; it seemed that another arduous, monotonous day lay ahead. But then, from behind the curtain of mist, we heard tinkling cowbells and a herdsman singing a lilting melody. The sun began to break through the mist, which lifted like a curtain. Swallows swooped around our heads, a tiny brown dolphin surfaced close to the kayak and water hyacinths twirled in the eddies made by our paddles. Buffaloes pulling carts loaded with whole families forded the river ahead of us, fishermen cast nets from the bank, women walked along with bundles of fodder on their heads. The sky was bright blue, the sun warm, and it was as if we'd emerged from one world into another.

Around midday, we stopped to wait for Bapi. His rudderless boat was hopelessly slow on flat water, and he was forever struggling along behind us. Despite this, he continued to cheerfully refer to himself as our "guide," something I was finding increasingly irritating.

"At this rate, we'll never get to Varanasi," I said peevishly. "Maybe it's not such a good idea having Bapi along."

"Don't be such a grouch!" retorted Dag. "He's great company, and he's not slowing us down that much. What's your problem?"

The problem was that I was jealous. For months now Dag and I had been traveling as a tight, self-contained unit, each of us the other's chief point of reference amidst a flurry of new experiences. But the dynamics of our relationship had been instantly changed by the presence of a third person. Dag was thrilled to have some male company, and an easy camaraderie had quickly developed between him and Bapi. At our campsites they prepared meals together, joked around, smoked bidis and swapped stories. To me, Bapi was courteous and considerate, and always insisted on relieving me of my washing up duties.

"I know you are busy with your note-writing, Maria!" he would say, cheerfully trudging off to scrub our pots in the cold river water.

But even such kind gestures failed to soften my resentment at how much of Dag's attention he was diverting from me, and I was often supercilious towards him.

"You're making a mistake by treating Bapi so harshly," Dag remonstrated. "He's more important to the success of this trip that you give him credit for."

As we talked we were drifting along beneath one of the river's "permanent" banks. Houses peeped between the trees on top of the twenty-foot-high bluff, and in front of it, rising up from the sand, was a skinny brick tower. Soon, children came careering down the bank. They were barefooted little ragamuffins with snotty noses and infected eyes, who splashed into the river, then screeched to a halt a few feet away from us, huddling together and giggling into their hands. From the bluff, adults beckoned to us. Anchoring the boat and clutching our Hindi phrase books, we went up to their village.

The houses were built of mud and dung and had pumpkins growing on the straw roofs. A *charpoi*—a wooden bed base with a woven rope mattress—was pulled out into the sunshine for us to sit on. Villagers pressed around: handsome, sharp-featured old men with leathery skin, young men holding babies and smoking bidis, women hiding their faces behind the ends of their saris. One of these women dunked a couple of stainless steel beakers into a clay pot filled with black, greasy water. She dried the beakers on her sari, then filled them with milky tea that she poured from a brass jug.

"*Bahut acchha,*" we said, sipping the tea. "Very good."

In Hindi, we asked some of our onlookers their names and the name of their village. Spurred on by success, Dag asked a man called Antram if he could tell us the purpose of the brick tower. There was a puzzled silence, then some whispered conferring. The men holding babies slid away and the children around our feet were yanked out of sight, but the remaining villagers pressed tightly around us. And the mood had changed; there was tension in the air.

"I think we'd better go," I whispered to Dag. We stood up.

"Sit down sir!" commanded Antram.

He produced a school exercise book and a pencil, and on the back page he wrote: "What is your name? Where are you coming from? What are you doing here?" Then he thrust the book and pencil at Dag.

The first two questions were simple to answer. The third was rather more problematic. What, after all, *were* we doing there?

Antram seemed to read our thoughts. *"What are you doing here, sir?"* he yelled at Dag.

Before Dag could reply, a familiar voice rang out.

"Hey, Dag!"

The crowd parted to reveal Bapi striding up the bank, his shorts flapping against his legs. "What's going on?"

"We're not sure," said Dag.

In the midst of my relief at seeing Bapi, I was struck by the fact that he was, indeed, our guide. Not in a physical sense, perhaps, but in situations like these, when he could help us bridge huge gulfs of language and culture. After a short conversation with Antram, he turned to us with a questioning look.

"These people are worried. They say you have been asking them about their children. They are thinking you want to take one of them with you."

Amid much relieved laughter, the misunderstanding was cleared up, we were brought more tea, and Antram explained about the tower. It was a well, and until a few years ago it had been in the center of the village. During each monsoon, part of Sherpur was swept away. Within a few months, the house we sat outside would probably be gone.

"That's terrible," I said.

When Bapi translated this, Antram smiled. "Not terrible. Holy Mother Ganga takes away, but she gives us fertile soil and good water. She is our life."

12

Center of Attention

Crows squabbled over the remains of our milk and rice breakfast as we broke camp. It was now eight days since we'd left Hardwar, and our progress had been pitifully slow.

One consolation was that the early mornings were losing their chilliness. By nine o'clock the sun had already begun to bleach the sky of its blue, and along the banks of the river, small turtles lay sunbathing on clods of earth. As we approached them, most plopped into the water, but some, perhaps fast asleep, stayed as they were, with their necks outstretched and their back flippers at right angles to their bodies. We were so engrossed in these creatures that at first we didn't notice the black smoke drifting toward us. Then we registered its acrid smell, its disquieting over-tones of fat left sizzling too long in the pan.

Coming around a bend in the river, we saw a burning pile of wood and dung. Inside it lay a body. Two men tended to the blaze with bamboo poles; about fifteen others stood to one side. On noticing our approach, they abandoned the pyre and ran to the water's edge, shouting and waving. They were wrapped up in dhotis and blankets, with only their faces and stick-thin legs show-ing. Some were very old, with wizened skin and eyes like birds. I turned around and called to Bapi, who was busy trying to catch a turtle on the end of his paddle, but he was out of earshot.

"Namaste," I said, pressing my hands together and raising them to my forehead.

"Namaste!" they all delightedly chorused.

There was a soft thump as the bow of our kayak ran onto a sub-merged sandbank. The current pushed us sideways, and in seconds we were firmly aground. Behind the men something on the fire cracked and popped. The wind shifted, and smoke began drifting and curling around us. As we struggled to push the boat off the sandbank with our paddles, ashes pattered against my face and caught in my eyelashes.

"We must join these people," said Bapi as he caught up with us.

"What?"

"They are requesting this."

A young man named Danbir spoke for the whole group. He was tall, rangy and rather dashing. He wore his blanket over one shoulder, like a toga, and he had a haughty way of holding up his long nose, as if sniffing the air. He invited us to sit with the men, and spread out a white cloth next to the tractor trailer that had brought the body, the mourners and the fuel down to the river-bank. Lumps of *gur*, crude cane sugar, were passed around. We were given the largest lumps, and mine was as big as a tennis ball. One of the old men sat very close to me, fixing me with his twinkling eyes as I began gnawing at the sweet, sticky stuff. Each time I took a break, he nodded vigorously, as if urging me on.

The body on the pyre, we learned, was that of Rishpal Singh. He had died only hours before, aged eighty-five. His eldest son, Sidraj, a man with a long, elegant face framed by a white cotton shawl, sat quietly talking to Bapi.

"Sidraj is requesting that we go back with him to his village," said Bapi. "He is saying that we have been sent to him as a blessing."

The village of Gessapur was five kilometers away from the river-bank. Going there would mean we'd lose a day, maybe more, putting us even further behind schedule. But Sidraj fixed us with a clear, steady gaze.

"He is saying that God took his father from him, and sent us as a blessing to comfort him in his grief," Bapi told us, and we found we couldn't refuse.

After two hours, the pyre was almost burned down, but a piece of backbone with something fleshy attached to it still lay among the coals. The mourners swept the lot into river and went in themselves for a ritual bath, holding their noses and immersing themselves three times. Then our boats were loaded onto the tractor trailer, and everyone squeezed around them. We drove along a bumpy track between fields of mustard, chili peppers, fennel, aubergine and wheat that were dazzlingly colorful after the pale vistas of the flood plain. The men laughed and chattered, as if returning from a party rather than a funeral.

Gessapur was a large village of over 800 people. Its houses were tightly packed along lanes of deeply rutted mud, and as we rumbled by we caught glimpses of buffalo tethered in courtyards and munching from mangers built into the walls, of old men sitting on charpois smoking hookahs, of women covering their faces with the ends of their saris and scuttling into dark, windowless rooms. Sidraj's house was on the edge of the village, next to fields spread with drying dung patties. Off its courtyard were a tiny kitchen with a dung-fired stove and two small rooms. Our boats and belongings were carried into one of the rooms; Bapi's kayak fitted inside, but the back half of the double kayak stuck out of the doorway. Sidraj led a buffalo into the courtyard, milked it, and presented us with beakers brimming with the warm, white liquid. I've never been partial to milk, even when it comes in sterilized bottles; the thought of drinking it straight from the udder turned my stomach. Watched by Sidraj's entire family and assorted neighbors, however, I had no option but to gulp it down and bravely smile.

Danbir decided that Dag and Bapi needed a shave, and took them off to find a barber. I was left in Sidraj's courtyard, surrounded by women. I sat on the charpoi, and they squatted on the ground around me, giggling at my sturdy sandals and my odd assortment of crumpled, dusty clothes. Over my thermal leggings and vest I was wearing a *kurta,* shorts and, for modesty's sake, my faded South Pacific sulu. The women had a long discussion, then one slipped away and returned a few minutes later with her arms full of magenta silk. I was led into a bedroom off the courtyard, a cool, dark place with mud walls. Six women crowded around me. Their glass bracelets tinkled as they deftly removed my clothes, and their fingers felt like cold marble against my skin. They first dressed me in a bodice that left my midriff bare—several bodices had to be rejected before one small enough was found, and this provoked a great deal of amusement. After tying a long cotton petticoat around my waist, they wrapped me in yard after yard of fine, rustling silk, which they expertly folded and tucked into a sari. My hair was combed and oiled, and a small round of red plastic, a *bindi*, was stuck onto my forehead to indicate my marital status. The three women stepped back to admire their handiwork, clapped their hands in delight, then led me off to be reunited with Dag.

Getting from one place to another in Gessapur proved to be a protracted affair. We usually managed only a few steps along one of the narrow streets before someone came flying out of a wooden door set into an ochre mud wall, dragged us into a courtyard and served us with sweet, milky tea and bowl after bowl of food. Everyone was curious about us and anxious to invite us to their homes, where we could properly be examined. But there was no such thing as privacy in Gessapur, as its flat roofs gave a grandstand view into neighboring courtyards. If one family treated us to potato pakora, the next-door family would immediately find out and feel prevailed upon to be seen offering us potato and onion pakora, and perhaps some milk curds as well. There was also the matter of *darshan*: as our journey was seen as holy and our arrival at the cremation far from coincidental, our presence was believed to be highly auspicious. We, in turn, felt duty-bound to force down the great quantities of food and drink offered to us, as any refusal was met with open dismay.

Back at Sidraj's house, I sat on the mud floor of the kitchen watching his wife Durta prepare mustard leaf curry and maize roti, a meal traditional to this area. From my afternoon in the village I'd gleaned something of the average daily workload of women like Durta. I'd seen how they meticulously swept mud floors and fireplaces, how they washed clothes by hand and pressed them with coal-filled irons, how they milked buffalo and churned the butter, how they collected dung and made it into fuel patties or mixed it with water to smear on the walls and floors of houses, how they spun and carded wool, how they winnowed lentil seeds and chopped up the fodder for the animals; all this as well as rearing children and catering to demanding husbands. And now, after such a day, pale, scrawny Durta, who had four living children and one on the way, was cooking, hunkered over a fire, feeding it with twigs and dung and constantly blowing on it to keep a strong enough flame burning. At the same time, she mixed maize flour and water, kneaded the dough and rolled small balls of it into flat rounds on a stone slab. She cooked these rotis one at a time over a dry pan, transferring them to the hot coals and leaving them there just long enough to puff out without burning. It was an operation I would have balked at in my high-tech kitchen, never mind this smoky little hut.

We ate in the courtyard, sitting on the charpois. Sidraj kept calling to his wife to bring us more rotis and to replenish our curry.

"Why doesn't Durta eat with us?" I asked Bapi.

"In the villages," he told me, "the women must wait until the men of the family have finished their food, and then they can eat what is left."

I'd just scooped up some curry with a piece of roti. It froze midway to my mouth.

"This is the tradition," he continued. "The women are treating their husbands like gods."

I began to protest, then stopped. Durta's life was regulated by age-old rules and rituals. For all I knew she might have been well aware of the iniquity of her situation, and of her powerlessness to change it, so who was I to breeze in, throw challenges around on her behalf, and then breeze out again? Without questioning Bapi further, I quietly finished my bowl of curry and refused the offer of more, hoping there would be some left for Durta.

"I am so tired," sighed Bapi, as we settled into our sleeping bags, "my eyelids are collapsing automatically."

We were in the same windowless room as the kayaks, squashed up against piles of dried dung patties. This had been where Sidraj's father had lived; Dag and I shared the charpoi on which he'd died the night before. A small oil lamp set in a wall niche threw weird shadows over the thatched ceiling. Outside, a mercury lamp hissed and spluttered, and Sidraj, who had insisted on acting as our night watchman, intoned a mantra. Despite its morbid associations, the room was cozy and snug, and we all fell asleep quickly.

"Chai! Chai!" yelled Sidraj, shaking our charpoi.

"What time is it?" I mumbled. It was pitch dark. Our little oil lamp had burned down, but outside the mercury lamp still hissed.

"Four-thirty," Dag told me.

"Chai! Chai!"

Sidraj was now at work on Bapi, who moaned and slid further

down inside his sleeping bag. We staggered to our feet, and Dag bent over Bapi and shook his shoulders.

"Chai! Chai!" he called into his ear. "Get up, we need an interpreter!"

"Really, I think you are learning Hindi very well," came his muffled reply.

Outside, we joined two men who were sitting on Sidraj's charpoi, watching him wrestle with a temperamental kerosene stove. Like them, we were wrapped in blankets, but they insisted that we snuggle beneath the heavy quilts that Sidraj had slept under, and one of them obligingly sat on my feet to warm them up. Once Sidraj had the stove going, he prepared a *chillum*, a cone-shaped marijuana pipe. From a pink plastic bag he took a handful of dried leaves and flower heads, poured a little water onto them, squeezed them between his palms, then stuffed them into the chillum. On top of the pipe he laid some glowing dung coals from a small fire close by, which seemed to have been made specifically for this purpose. With a damp cloth around the end of the chillum, he put it to his lips, inhaled, then passed it on. Mercifully, being female excluded me from this ritual. But it was a strong drug: the second-hand smoke, or perhaps just the soporific atmosphere that quickly developed, made the already strange situation seem quite bizarre. Dag, meanwhile, seemed to have suddenly mastered the basics of Hindi, and he happily chatted with the men and interpreted the conversation for me.

"Sidraj wants to know if we slept well. I told him it was the best sleep we'd had in ages."

"I wish it had been longer. When did you learn all that Hindi vocabulary?"

"I dunno. I can just tell what he's saying."

We drank cup after cup of sweet milky chai while two more chillums went round and a sepia dawn crept over us. From time to time Sidraj yelled into the hut, but he got only groans in reply. At 6:30, a bleary-eyed Bapi finally emerged.

"You know what Sidraj was shouting?" he asked Dag.

"He was telling you to get up," Dag confidently answered.

"No! He was asking why you got up so early! It was not necessary, he only came to ask if you wanted bed tea!"

The problem with drinking so much tea was that I soon needed to dispose of it, and Sidraj's house didn't have a latrine.

The night before, under cover of darkness, I'd slipped away beyond a field of drying dung and into a thicket of bamboo. But now I couldn't reach the end of the field unobserved and once I practically stumbled over a man who was squatting down next to his *chembu,* a brass pot filled with water he would clean himself with after defecating. Despondently, I wandered along a lane, listening to noses and throats being vigorously cleared behind courtyard walls. Some women overtook me, carrying on their heads baskets filled with steaming dung. One of them yelled what sounded like an oath at a house, and seconds later the gate opened and a head popped around it.

"Garam chai!" the head cried. "Hot tea!"

A hand shot out and I was whisked inside.

As this was one of the wealthier houses of the village, it had two courtyards, three rooms for living and sleeping in, a bath house and, to my great relief, a latrine. Although it was merely a hole in the ground behind a low mud-brick wall, to me, at that moment, it was utterly luxurious. Yet even here I wasn't totally alone—a tethered buffalo with pieces of grass stuck to its wet nose peered over the wall to watch what I was doing.

It proved impossible to leave Gessapur that day, as Danbir had organized a tractor to take us and his extended family to a religious festival that was being held some miles away. He'd also arranged that we should move to the house of some of his richer relatives where, he said, we would be more comfortable. I was relieved, as much for my own sake as for that of Sidraj's wife, for whom we were undoubtedly adding to an already gargantuan workload. Dag, however, was crestfallen. He had loved sleeping by the dung pile and chatting with the boys at 4:30 a.m. Sidraj was as gracious as ever, insisting that as we were now part of his family we could wander where we wished, but his house would always be our home. Leaving our boats in his care, we followed Danbir to our new abode, which we finally reached after six stops on the way and innumerable cups of chai.

Rahul Choudhary met us at the gate of his family's outer courtyard. For our benefit he'd gotten dressed up in his best clothes: tight-fitting polyester trousers, a sports jacket and blue plastic shoes.

"This is machines," he said, pointing to the Enfield motorbike and tractor, both covered by muddy tarpaulins, that were parked next to the cow and buffalo mangers. Rahul was twenty-two and unmarried. His elder brother, Shiv Kumar, was traditionally dressed, and more concerned with showing off his one-year-old daughter, who had eyes ringed with kohl to ward off evil spirits, and silver bells hanging from chains around her plump ankles and wrists.

"This is baby," said Rahul, pointing to his niece. "This is arm. This is leg."

Since their father had died three years before, Shiv Kumar and Rahul had run the household. Their 150 acres of farmland were worked by laborers; they had two house servants, and they were cooked for and cosseted by Ewartidevi, their mother, and Rita, Shiv Kumar's wife.

In the inner courtyard, an old servant in a thin cotton sari used ash to scrub brass pots to a high shine. Next to her, Rita filled buckets with water from a hand pump. In the kitchen, Ewartidevi was stoking up a fire to warm the water so we could wash in the bath house, a small room with a drain hole in the floor. My offers of help were rebuffed: like the men, I was to sit and be waited on hand and foot.

Some bricks had fallen from the wall on one side of the courtyard, and several of the neighbors' faces were pressed close to this makeshift window. Their eyes followed me as I was led off by Rita to be dressed in a pink sari. For a time, their interest switched to Rita, who washed my clothes in a bucket and held up each dripping garment for general inspection. The sight of my knickers provoked much ribald cackling, but I managed to regain the audience's attention by inserting my contact lenses. The family crowded around to watch this operation, and the neighbors, no longer able to contain themselves, raced up their stairs, across the roof and down into the Choudhary's courtyard. By the time they arrived, both lenses were in place. I was persuaded to repeat the procedure, and it was only after I had removed and reinserted my lenses a total of six times that we were allowed to set off for the religious fair.

This was the women's big day, the chance for them to escape from the courtyards and the smoky kitchens and do a spot of socializing. As the tractor bounced through the narrow streets of the village, more and more women climbed aboard; by the time we were out on the plain, rumbling across a brick road, I was well protected from the chilling wind by a solid press of laughing, singing bodies.

For most of the seven-mile journey the road followed the Ganges Canal, an uninspiring stretch of slimy green water with concrete embankments. From half a mile away we could see a bridge which led across it to the site of the festival. As we approached, traffic from surrounding villages built up until the road was a muddled, noisy confusion of tractor trailers, buffalo carts, bicycles, scooters and thousands of people. We parked at the side of the road, and as I awkwardly clambered down from the trailer, Ewartidevi took hold of a corner of my sari. Pulling me firmly along behind her, she launched into the human tide heading across the bridge.

The fair was an annual celebration of Kali, the goddess of destruction, who is usually depicted garlanded with skulls. Despite her fearsome reputation, Kali's temple was an innocuous pink building atop a small hill. Beneath it was the fair, row after row of stalls selling sweets, fried vegetables, betel leaves and nuts, and an astonishing array of gaudy trivia: plastic bangles, combs, mirrors, hairpieces, lacy padded bras, cheap make-up and plastic potted plants. There were snake charmers, holy men giving blessings in return for alms and a greasily handsome singer belting out religious songs. Bapi ran excitedly among the stalls, buying gifts for all the members of the Choudhary family.

"Maria, stop, let me buy you something, too!" he cried. But Ewartidevi still had me in tow, and, tripping on the hem of my sari, I stumbled through the melee with her as we made our way to the temple.

On the steps an excited crowd was jostling its way toward the double doors of Kali's shrine. Everyone carried offerings: chapatis, bowls of milk, bottles of ghee, sweets. Close to the doors, the excitement mounted to near hysteria and some people began throwing their offerings onto the flat temple roof, where two pujaris dressed in pink and splattered with food fielded the solid offerings, such as chapatis, and dodged the wetter missiles, such as milk and curds. From inside the temple came a deafening clamor of bells, gongs and shouting. By standing on tiptoe and peering over heads, I could see to the far door, from where worshippers were emerging with their hair plastered in ghee and curds. My feet, I realized, were sinking into a sticky goo, and when the man in front of me was doused in milk I decided it was time to retreat.

Ewartidevi had the same idea. With an impressive backhand she flung her rotis at the roof, then elbowed a passageway for us back down the steps.

The true goal of the day was the picnic lunch on the tractor trailer. Women shared out rotis and vegetable sabzee, or stew, and gossiped with people from other villages. All the men, including Dag and Bapi, had their cheeks stuffed with paan, leaf-wrapped bundles of betel nut, spices, lime and opium which were causing their eyes to glaze and their teeth to turn a nasty shade of rust red. Rahul was in his element, cheerfully answering an onslaught of questions about his Western guests. He already knew the answers to queries on our origins, our professions and our journey. But when it came to how old we were and how many children we had, he first had to check with us.

"I'm thirty-five and Maria's thirty-nine," Dag told him. "And we have no children."

Rahul's face was a picture of horrified disbelief. He turned to Bapi for affirmation of this untenable information. Bapi, however, was equally flabbergasted.

"Maria, you are thirty-nine? How can this be? My mother is not so old as that!"

My age and my childlessness were the subjects of furious debate all the way back to Gessapur. The women around me yelled the news to the occupants of other tractor trailers and bullock carts. I was pointed at and given long, sympathetic looks. I sat, draped in a sari and wrapped in a blanket, feeling thoroughly confused. In comparison to these women, I was rich, privileged and with freedoms beyond their wildest dreams: I'd chosen my husband, I could earn my own living, direct my own destiny, control my fertility. And yet they felt desperately sorry for me, because I lacked the one thing that gave their life some purpose and meaning—a child. Whatever successes I had were negated by the tragic fact that I was barren. I could, I suppose, have tried to explain to them that in my culture it was possible to find other means of status and fulfillment, other insurances against old age. I could have admitted that I had chosen to be childless. And yet I said none of these things. I watched Ewartidevi comforting her granddaughter with a nipple, contentedly cooing at the baby and tickling it under the chin, and I wondered what in fact I was doing, at almost forty, dragging a boat around the world instead of being at home and raising children. Unable to answer this to myself, it was hopeless trying to communicate it to the women, so I simply nodded when they told me to that I should pray to Goddess Ganga for a child, and return next year to Gessapur with a baby in my arms.

Back at the Choudharys' house, we ate dinner sitting on the mud floor of the kitchen, while Ewartidevi and Rita flipped rotis straight from the fire into our bowls of dhal. At seven o'clock, Dag and Bapi went to visit Sidraj, but I was exhausted and started getting ready for bed. My hopes for sleep were dashed by the arrival of Mr. Succha Singh, the local vet. He had heard that Dag was also a vet, and had come to discuss with him the matter of a sick buffalo. Dag was sent for, and in the meantime I was asked to entertain Mr. Singh. We sat in the bedroom that Dag, Bapi and I were sharing with Rahul. Mr. Singh comfortably sprawled out on one of the four beds, smoking pungent tobacco from an enormous hookah. I sat opposite him, and the family and neighbors gathered around to watch our exchange. For a few minutes, the vet simply puffed on his gurgling hookah, fixing me with an intense stare through the billowing clouds of smoke. Then, in a loud, barking voice, he announced, "Economics is the science of wealth!" I blinked at him.

"Economics is the science of wealth!" he yelled.

"Oh," I said. "Yes."

"Philosophy," he said, as if this was a statement in itself.

"Yes."

"Sociopoligy."

"You mean sociology?" I asked.

He glowered at me.

"Yes!"

There followed a long, pregnant pause, during which he drew deeply on his hookah.

"You have lallergy from the government?" he finally asked.

"Pardon?"

"The Indian government!" he shouted. "The service civil!"

"The civil service?"

"Yes! Do you have lallergy?" The crowd tightened around us, bristling with tension.

"I don't know," I said.

By now Mr. Singh appeared quite exasperated. "Lallergy service civil the Indian government! Your boat the Ganga! Lallergy!"

Inspiration struck. "Permission?" I hesitantly inquired.

"Yyyyesss!" he shrieked, showering me with spit.

"We have a letter of permission," I told him, "from the Ministry of Tourism."

"Very good!"

The crowd sighed with relief, and Mr. Singh grinned triumphantly.

Shortly afterwards, Dag arrived back from his session with Sidraj. Despite his rather glazed state, he listened carefully to Mr. Singh, who didn't actually want his opinion, but rather wished to be seen and heard discussing the matter with him.

"And I am thinking," the vet loudly concluded, "that this buffalo is having foot and mouth disease!"

Only the bubbling of Mr. Singh's hookah broke the long silence, while Dag cast around for something tactful to say about this wildly inaccurate diagnosis.

"I'm not sure if . . ." he began.

Mr. Singh's eyes narrowed dangerously. Dag stopped, and reformulated his sentence.

"I have no experience of buffalo," he said. "But Mr. Singh has much experience."

"This is right!" shrieked Singh. "Exactly right!"

"And what will you prescribe?" Dag asked him.

"Vitamins!" he shouted.

Two more days passed before we managed to leave Gessapur. While Dag and Bapi went off wild boar hunting and visiting other villages with the men of the family, I stayed in the courtyard with the women. It was a fly-ridden place, and in the summer months must have been unbearably hot, but it was where Ewartidevi and Rita spent most of their lives. Keeping their women closeted at home while servants shopped and laborers worked the fields was how families like the Choudharys showed off their wealth. My presence was a welcome diversion from this monotonous existence, and women from other courtyards also flocked to see me, arriving via the system of interlocking roofs and stairways. For almost every minute of every day I was surrounded by curious onlookers with a very different sense of personal space than mine. This was particularly the case with the older women; they blithely felt my breasts or lifted up my sari to have a good look at my body, they picked through the contents of my clothes and toiletry bags, they paged through my notebooks. While I endeavored to graciously submit myself to such intense scrutiny, I began to look forward to the relative privacy we would enjoy back on the river. And while I was reluctant to leave the company of the women and to exchange this pampering and relative comfort for slogging through sandbanks and camping in mud, I was becoming increasingly anxious about the fact that we should really be continuing with our journey.

Dag, however, was in his element and in no hurry to leave Gessapur. He was adopting the characteristics of a rural Indian, wearing a kurta, smoking bidis, peppering his conversation with "Acchha" while waggling his head from side to side, spitting on the ground and blowing his nose into his fingers. Bapi, too, was happily settled in. Considering that he was a thoroughly urbanized, Westernized and secularized Indian, he had an unusually strong affection for rural life, and his empathy with village people opened doors and hearts to us everywhere we went with him. The downside of this was that he was forever in league with the villagers, trying to entice us to stop, to accept tea, to rest, to stay another night. All of which was delightful, but at this rate it was looking increasingly unlikely that we'd ever get to Varanasi. On our fourth evening in Gessapur I put my foot down and said quite firmly that we had to leave the following morning.

News of this decision quickly spread, and within the hour we received a visit from the school committee. This formidable posse of elderly men in dhotis and plastic slip-on shoes marched into the Choudharys' courtyard and sat facing us on a charpoi. We'd met them once before, on our first day in Gessapur, when we'd made a donation to the school of forty-one rupees.

"You are a rich family," said the leader, a stern man in a white Nehru cap.

The Choudharys watched and listened carefully. As tradition demanded, both Rita and Ewartidevi had covered the bottom half of their faces, but above the silk their eyes were blazing with fury.

"Our school is poor," continued the man. "You must be giving more money—at least one thousand rupees!"

There was a moment of shocked silence. A thousand rupees!

By local standards it was an exorbitant amount. We had to consider village politics, for by being particularly generous to one family or faction, we would arouse considerable jealousies. What we didn't know at this point, but should have guessed by the Choudharys' glowering faces, was that the school committee was widely renowned for its venality. Quickly, Bapi stepped in as interpreter and mediator. He explained that because of the vulnerability of our mode of transport we were not carrying a lot of cash.

"Tell him," said Dag, "that we will donate another hundred rupees."

"That's too much," Bapi replied. "If you want to give more, make it sixty rupees so that the total amount is one hundred and one rupees."

The stern man, understanding the gist of this conversation, yelled in fury at Bapi, remonstrating with him for trying to persuade us to donate less. At this, Ewartidevi could no longer contain herself, and she launched into an attack, first at the committee for marching uninvited into her house, and then at us for being foolish enough to consider giving these criminals a single rupee more. Bapi talked and soothed and translated until an agreement was reached. Sixty rupees were handed over, another receipt was written out, and Dag shook hands with the five men.

"Very good, very kind," said the man in the Nehru cap. "Now, tell me, sir, is it true that in North America sex is free?"

We left Gessapur at dawn. Ewartidevi and Rita looked stricken as we gave them gifts and made our farewells, and I had to blink back my tears.

"Maria, no cry!" insisted Rahul. "Cry bad luck!"

At Sidraj's house, after more chai and a final chillum, we loaded our boats and baggage on to Danbir's buffalo cart. As it rumbled along the village lanes, people ran from their courtyards, heaping us with their blessings and exhorting us to return. With a strong sense of loss, we slowly made our way through the fertile fields and back to the empty expanse of the flood plain.

13

Full Immersion

We lay in some long grass on a ledge halfway up a clay bluff. A pale, hazy sun warmed us and a breeze rippled the surface of the river murmuring thirty feet below.

"What's the date?" I asked Dag.

He checked his watch. "Valentine's Day!"

Our eyes met as we shared the same thought. Bapi was about forty-five minutes behind us. Dare we take advantage of this, the most private moment we'd had in two weeks? Before we could even reach for each other, however, the peace of the morning was rent by a burst of shouting. Peering over the ledge we saw three men hurrying toward our beached kayak. Half a mile back, we'd paddled past some large, cone-shaped heaps of dung patties stacked right on the edge of the high embankment and covered with straw to protect them from rain. Although this was the sign of a village close by, we'd decided to carry on for fear of being waylaid by Indian hospitality so soon after leaving Gessapur.

By the time we reached the kayak, the three men were hopping about in excitement.

"*Baba!*" they cried, pointing to the path they had just run down. "*Baba!*"

Baba is the familiar name given to *saddhus,* or mendicant holy men. Along the river we'd encountered several of them, in orange robes and wooden sandals, their hair wild and their foreheads marked with sandalwood paste according to which Hindu god they worshipped. The saddhu these men took us to had forehead markings in the shape of a trident, Shiva's symbol. His hair, like Lord Shiva's, from which the Ganges is said to have originated, was matted into waist-length dreadlocks. He had a long, straggly beard, and he was wrapped in saffron cloth and a biscuit-colored shawl. In front of him, a tomato held open the pages of a holy book, and he was reading in a singsong voice to a rapt audience of men from the nearby village. Our arrival did not seem to surprise him in the least; he motioned for us to sit down and called to a young man who sat tending a cook fire outside a brick hut to make chai. Beyond the hut, and surrounded by tulsi and neem trees, was a small Shiva temple with pink walls and turrets and heavy wooden doors. The saddhu, whose name was Baba Amardas, had apparently found a temporary resting place, and it was soon obvious that he was inviting us to share it with him for the night.

"What do you think?" asked Dag, looking hopefully at me. I gazed around. From our high vantage point we could see the Ganga looping across the flood plain, and the splashes of green and yellow fields around the ochre tones of the nearby village. After days spent inside walled courtyards, it was good to be out in the open, and with such a view. And then there was Bapi to consider, no doubt weary after four hours of hard paddling. Baba Amardas was smiling, showing off even white teeth and waggling his head from side to side.

"Acchha? Acchha?"

By the time Bapi arrived, our kayak had been carried up the steep bank and set on the holy ground by the temple.

Before long, Baba Amardas produced a chillum. According to Hindu mythology, Shiva spent a lot of time smoking marijuana, and the Shivite saddhus we met all seemed to be striving to follow their lord's example. While the chillum went around, through Bapi I asked the baba to tell us about himself. He was from Assam, but he couldn't say when he'd left there or at what age, as when he became a saddhu he'd renounced and "forgotten" everything of his former life, including his name. He had been at this spot for some weeks, and complained that the villagers were looking after him too well, bringing him too much food, and that he could pray better when he was hungry. By this time the chillum had gone round several times, and the baba was in full flow, without any need of my prompts.

"Oh God, I don't believe it," said Bapi. "He is talking now in rhyme, and he is saying that the chillum is his rifle, and he is loading it with ganja and aiming it to heaven in a salute!"

Baba Amardas broke wind, then turned and made a comment to Bapi, who went into convulsions of laughter, clutching his sides and rolling on the ground. The villagers, who had not been partaking of the chillum, looked rather alarmed by this irreverent behavior.

"Oh God! No! I don't believe it!" gasped Bapi. "He's a crazy baba!"

"What, Bapi? What did he say?"

"He said sometimes when he lights his weapon it fires out of the wrong end!"

And that, for a while, was the end of Bapi as a useful translator, as he spent much of the next eighteen hours either laughing or asleep.

Leaving Bapi with Baba Amardas, Dag and I walked into the village. The winding path took us through a hummocky landscape and past gnarled trees with parrots squawking and fluttering in the branches. Shinkiteela village was half the size of Gessapur, and its houses had a fairy tale quality about them, with rounded steps and lopsided doorways, blue and white friezes painted onto dung and mud walls, and iridescent peacock feathers hanging in windows. But the people who gathered around us were pitifully poor. Children with ragged clothes, mud-caked feet and tousled hair peeked out from behind their parents, and one of the mothers, still in her teens, held on her hip a small child with horrifying burns. Three days before, we ascertained, the girl had fallen into a cooking fire, and now her leg was covered with blackened crusts, some of which had rubbed off, exposing raw flesh that oozed thick yellow pus.

To the dismay of the villagers, who obviously thought we were fleeing from the sight of this dreadful wound, we hurried back to the kayak to collect some first-aid supplies. Baba Amardas was now singing, one of the village men was playing a small harmonium which he pumped with his left hand while working the keyboard with his right, and Bapi was doing some impressive tabla-like drumming on a metal plate. His conversation, however, had become inane.

"I asked the baba for this plate and he was thinking I was wanting his food! It is so funny!"

"Bapi, come with us, we need you to translate."

"Oh God! It is not possible! I cannot walk!"

Flies crawled around the child's eyes as she stared unflinchingly at Dag while he cleaned and dressed her wound. By now we were surrounded by aspiring patients, most of them elderly men with no obvious afflictions. They coughed theatrically, or grimaced and patted their stomachs, or hobbled to and fro with pronounced limps.

"The old buggers," said Dag. "They're put out because two females got all the attention."

Inside Baba Amardas's hut Dag cooked a sabzee over our kerosene stove, and the villagers bought us rotis and milk curds. The baba blessed all the food by sprinkling it with Ganges water that he'd carried from the river in a brass pot. He ate voraciously and messily, with many appreciative burps.

"The baba says the day after tomorrow is an inauspicious day to travel," Bapi told me.

"Why?"

There was a brief and giggly exchange between them.

"He is saying this is a holy place, and if you are staying here you must tolerate all sorts of holy shit."

"Bapi, he didn't say that!"

"He did! I swear!"

After dinner I left the three men and crawled into our tent, which we'd erected a little distance from the hut. I drifted in and out of sleep, only dimly conscious of the raucous laughter and singing that went on far into the night.

At first light, the baba started moving around, muttering his mantras, burping and farting. He emerged from the hut wearing only a dhoti and carrying a brass bucket, and set off towards the river. I followed at a discreet distance. His puja was a simple one: he scooped up water in his palms, let it slowly trickle through his fingers, and held his upturned face and hands to the rising sun. Praying aloud, he filled the bucket and returned to the temple, which was now a glowing violet color. Three times he walked around it, sprinkling water on the holy ground, on the revered tulsi trees, on our kayak. Swinging open the heavy doors, he stepped inside and began to sing, his voice reverberating around the domed ceiling. Over the *lingam,* a phallic stone symbolizing the creative aspect of Shiva, he poured water, scattered marigolds and wafted burning incense sticks. Still muttering prayers, he backed out of the temple and pulled the heavy doors so that they banged shut with a sepulchral boom. Turning to face the Ganga, he blew on a conch, three long blasts which resonated across the flood plain, made the hair on my neck stand on end and managed to wake even Bapi and Dag.

Stripes of vivid red and yellow sandalwood paste were freshly daubed on Baba Amardas's forehead, and his dreadlocks were piled on top of his head and wrapped in orange cloth. Squinting against the bright morning sunshine, he bent to touch and bless our boats before we carried on with our journey.

"He is saying," said Bapi blearily, "that our pilgrimage is cleansing our hands, our food and our water. He is saying also that ahead there are bandits and we must take care."

I handed him a donation inside one of the plastic Ziploc bags that he had so admired the day before. His eyes registered surprise, his head waggled from side to side, and he smiled. And then, to my own considerable surprise, I knelt and placed my forehead on his feet to receive his blessing.

Toward late afternoon of our twelfth day on the Ganga, we reached the town of Anupshahr. According to Bapi's estimates, we were about a third of the way to Varanasi. The last section of the river had been delightful, with deep water, strong currents, warm sun and the wind at our backs. We'd sped by constantly changing scenes, each one a cameo in itself: a lush green village with young palms and ancient peepul trees; a temple that was literally crumbling into the river; buffalo contentedly lolling in the water while children scrubbed them down; fishermen casting nets from wooden boats; a sweep of sculpted dunes where three women stood holding up freshly washed saris to dry in the wind, so that yards and yards of emerald, azure and scarlet silk flapped like giant flags against the silvery sand.

Temples lined the bank at the town of Anupshahr, and on one of the ghats, the steps leading down to the river, a pujari sat and watched our approach as if it was the most normal thing in the world.

"If you are wanting to buy toilet paper," he told us, "I am sorry but you will not be finding it in Anupshahr."

There was a pause while we considered this information.

"We are looking for a safe place to spend the night," said Dag.

The pujari waggled his head. "Acchha. You will be finding it here, sir."

He told us we could store our boats in the ashram next to the temple, and that there was a room on the roof where we could sleep. The room was a bare cell with a glassless window. Stuck onto a nail between two bricks was a garishly colored picture of the boy Krishna with his hand in a bowl of milk curds. Outside, on the parapet, monkeys with black faces and white ruffs tugged at the zip of our red sack, and one of them bared its yellow fangs at me when I tried to shoo it away.

"These are holy monkeys," Bapi remonstrated. "You must be respectful of them."

Beyond the ashram, pigs snuffled in the open drain that ran down the middle of Anupshahr's main street. At a chai stall, we sat on a plank propped between two oil cans and drank tea from small terra-cotta beakers. It was customary to use these beakers only once, and around our feet the discarded ones lay broken and crumbling into the mud. The stall's owner squatted on top of his adobe oven, fanning the fire inside and adding more milk, tea, water and gur to a smoke-blackened pot. Before long, a crowd had formed around us, and soon the narrow street was congested with people, scooters, rickshaws and pigs. Two gun-toting policemen came wading through to see what was causing such a commotion. After shooing away the onlookers to a reasonable distance, they joined us on the plank.

"When you reach Narora," one of them told us, "you must be stopping for a picnic. It is not far and indeed a beautiful place, the biggest hydroelectricity dam in Asia!"

"Madam," the other asked me, curiously eyeing my kayak jacket. "Why is it that foreigners always are having so many pockets?"

Later that night, I crept down from the roof, hoping to find a private spot that I could use as a toilet. I was loath to follow Bapi's suggestion to "Do it into the river" or the pujari's vague instructions to use a nearby alleyway, "Women on left and men on right!" From one of the temples came frenzied chanting: *"Hare Ram Hare Ram Ram Hare Hare! Hare Krishna Hare Krishna Krishna Krishna Hare Hare!"* I considered going in there and asking about a latrine, then thought better of it. It was after midnight, and the sight of a western woman in pink long johns might not be a welcome one. Finding a place to pee and shit, at home a simple, straightforward matter, had for months now presented me with a daily dilemma. It had been bad enough in the Solomon Islands, where there were crocodiles, centipedes and snakes to worry about, but at that moment I would have happily waded into a mangrove swamp instead of skulking around these shadowy streets, hoping in vain to come across a few bushes. Finally, I ventured into the alleyway, only to be chased out by a pack of snarling dogs. I gave up, and went back to bed in a foul humor.

But at dawn, when I stepped out of our tiny room, my bad mood evaporated. The plain stretched away, awash with an amber light. Music blared from the temples, incense drifted up from the pujas taking place on the ghats. A woman stood praying in the river, her maroon sari floating on its bronze surface. A barber tonsured a three-year-old Brahmin boy, carefully leaving one long strand of hair on his crown. The boy's mother placed some of the shorn hair on a banana leaf and offered it to the river. Men wearing dhotis and the sacred thread of Brahmins across their bare chests sat meditating in perfect lotus positions. A cow wandered about the ghat, and people pressed their foreheads between its horns to receive its blessing. Also in progress were secular affairs. Women rinsed out basketfuls of lentils, washed cooking pots and clothes, or squatted on the ghats, rubbing their heels against the rough stone to remove hard skin. Men lathered themselves from head to foot with soap and cleaned their teeth with twigs.

Presently, over all this activity a new light was cast, as the red orb of the sun peeped over the horizon. The bathers turned their faces to it, and held their palms upwards. Quickly, before I had time to reconsider, I wrapped myself in my sulu and hurried down to the women's ghat. A woman in a wet sari that clung to her body as revealingly as if she were naked reached out her hand to me. She drew me into the cold water until I was chest deep, and my bare feet had left the steps and were sinking into mud. With her free hand she held her nose and nodded at me to do the same. Shutting my eyes and holding my breath, I ducked my head beneath the surface for the ritual three immersions.

Our pujari friend smeared my forehead with sandalwood paste and gave me a prasad of blessed sweets. Sitting cross-legged on a wooden table, he recorded in a large ledger my name, my act of worship and the merit I had accrued towards gaining a place in heaven. Around him were puja items for sale: camphor, marigolds, coconuts and red cloths, as well as combs and mirrors that he rented out to worshippers so they could tidy up their hair after bathing. He offered me one of the greasy combs, but I couldn't face using it. My first full immersion in the Ganga had been experience enough for one day.

By noon we'd reached Rajghat, a muddy pilgrimage site where hundreds of red and yellow flags fluttered above temporary straw shacks. A railway bridge spanned the river, and beneath it men stood neck-deep in water, their heads moving almost imperceptibly from side to side. It wasn't, as I first thought, some form of devotion we had not yet encountered.

"People throw money offerings to Ganga from the train windows," explained Bapi. "And these men are making a living by looking for the money with their toes."

To get past the huge, hulking structure of Narora Barrage, we employed the services of a man and his handcart. The cart was a hopelessly rickety affair made of a few short planks tacked onto a scrap metal frame and resting on four flat bicycle tires. We loaded the boats and baggage on top of it and set off on the long portage, with Dag holding one end of the double kayak and Bapi the other, the cart groaning and jolting beneath the weight and all four wheels wobbling around in different directions.

Narora, as the policeman in Anupshahr had intimated, was indeed a popular picnic site. There were lawns and flower beds, swings and roundabouts for children and a 3-D ceramic display of the course of the Ganges from source to sea, with Narora Barrage and power station prominently displayed. And there were scores of well-dressed Indian tourists who looked up from their picnics on the parched grass to watch in amazement the uncertain progress of our cart. A group of urbane youths in Western clothes latched onto us.

"Excuse me, what is the exact height of your husband?" one asked me.

"Six feet two inches."

"That is the exact height of Amitabh Bachchan, India's famous movie star. Are you knowing this man? His attempts to enter political life ended in the most terrible scandal."

Walking toward us from the opposite direction was a frail old pilgrim. He was wrapped in jute sacking, carried a staff, and looked for all the world like some ancient prophet. At the sight of us he opened wide his toothless mouth, and hooted with loud, merry laughter.

We made it through the park, past all the picnickers, across a busy road, over a bridge and to the far side of the barrage, where, to our collective dismay, we saw trucks bowling over a wide plain, raising clouds of white dust and easily fording a shallow, shrunken river.

14

The Bouncing Baba

Once more blighted by low water and submerged sandbanks, for the next three days we pushed and poled our way downstream more than we paddled. As if taunting us with the ridiculousness of our situation, men crossed the river ahead of us on bicycles, and the saddhus walking along the bank easily overtook us. I tried to block out the discomfort and the frustration by turning my thoughts to home. I wondered how our cats were, if our fruit trees had survived the frost. I pictured our house, lashed by winter winds and rain—and suddenly the drain pipes, or rather the lack of them, popped into my head.

"When we get back to Canada," I told Dag, "let's get all the jobs on the house done straight away."

"Jobs?"

"Yes, you know, like the drain pipes, and the—"

"Drain pipes? Is this a joke?"

"No! Look, if we don't get on with things like the drain pipes, the house will be falling down around our heads before it's even finished."

"Why the hell are you worrying about drain pipes when we're in the middle of—"

He was interrupted by a soft thump as a submerged sandbank snared us.

"Instead of coming on this trip," said Dag through gritted teeth as we struggled to push the boat free, "we could have spent a year finishing the house and inviting all the neighbors over to admire our nice new drain pipes."

At that precise moment, standing knee-deep in mud and with the wind filling my ears with sand, it didn't seem such a bad option.

"And maybe," he continued sarcastically, "we could have mowed the lawn every Sunday and bought plastic garden furniture and one of those lovely striped umbrellas—"

"Actually," I interrupted, as I heaved at the boat, "I'd like to buy a lawn mower."

"A lawn mower?" he spluttered.

At Dag's insistence, we'd left our field-sized lawn in its natural state.

"Last summer I had to hack my way through the long grass to get to the vegetable patch."

"And I suppose you'll want to put weed killer down as well?" he cried, glaring at me across the cockpit. "And how about a few garden gnomes while you're at it?"

"I just want to mow the bloody thing!" I yelled back.

"What's the matter?" cried Bapi, who was stuck behind us.

"Oh, nothing," I replied. "We're just having a domestic squabble."

"I'm about to murder my wife," Dag told him. "And then I'm going to cremate her on the riverbank."

"I am very sorry about this, Maria!" said Bapi. "But at least you will be going straight to heaven."

The river got wider and deeper, but as if reminding itself not to hurry, it snaked about the plain in dramatic loops and bends, so that often we found ourselves paddling back in the direction from which we'd just come. At the end of the third day, we were reconciling ourselves to yet another desolate campsite when, beyond the gray-green water and over the shoals of silvery sand, people appeared as if in a mirage. First just a handful of them, running toward us, their saris and striped *lungis* fluttering against the white sand and the sapphire sky. Then more and more sprang up, until a big crowd was bearing down on us. An evil-looking man with bloodshot protruding eyes and stubby black teeth reached us first. He grabbed our kayak by the rudder and began dragging us to shore. Dag jumped out of his cockpit to fend off this unwanted attention, but within seconds the man was just one of over a hundred people, pressing in from all sides, yelling at us in Hindi, wildly gesticulating, pushing and shoving us in their excitement. Bapi and his boat were out of sight, lost somewhere in the melee, and I was hit by a flash of panic: we were hopelessly outnumbered and at the mercy of this near hysterical throng. Suddenly heads turned away from us and bodies moved back, and a tall, strongly built saddhu with fierce eyes and a black beard appeared, beating people away with a bamboo pole and hurling handfuls of sand into their faces.

"My God!" cried Bapi, appearing at our side. "I believed I was about to suffocate!"

The saddhu promptly began berating Bapi. He was with a theater group that for the holy month of Magh was traveling along the Ganges giving four-day-long performances of the *Ramayana*, one of the Hindus' epic poems. Much to his chagrin, we had ruined that day's performance, which was taking place on a high bank beyond the shoal. A rumor of foreigners on the river in a strange boat had spread like wildfire, and the audience had abandoned the play to seek us out. Nonetheless, he invited us to come and spend the night at the troupe's encampment. He turned to the crowd, now shaking sand out of hair and lungis a safe distance away, and marshaled it into carrying our boats up the embankment.

The stage was a freestanding, rickety affair constructed from rough planks and bamboo and festooned with ropes and pulleys to raise and lower six hand-painted backdrops. To one side was a row of temporary straw huts. We were given one of these to sleep in, and our kayaks and belongings were laid down outside it. Sabzee and rotis were brought for us, and ginger-flavored tea. While we ate and drank, our saddhu, whom Bapi nicknamed the Bouncing Baba, tirelessly ran about. He chased curious children away, thwacked the dogs that mooched around, ordered food to be brought to us and supervised the lighting of a fire fueled with straw pulled from the roofs of the huts. The actors, musicians and saddhus gathered to stare at us, and eventually the Bouncing Baba settled down to join them.

After three days of struggling with sandbanks, we were worn out, and retired early to our shelter. Unfortunately, it was open fronted, so our audience simply shifted position to continue watching us. Rather pointedly, Dag hung up one of our blankets, but the men simply craned their necks to see around it. Minutes after we'd settled down, a public address system crackled to life—from where it was powered we never discovered—and strident religious music blasted across the camp. It went on for a couple of hours, until it was replaced by the more humdrum sounds of chanting, talking, snoring and dog fights. A rat nosed about the hut, and once ran across our legs. An hour or so before dawn there was a new and haunting disturbance. It started in the distance and got steadily closer and louder: female voices, flat and childishly high, singing the same refrain over and over again. I lay in my sleeping bag, imagining a line of women with brass bowls on their heads, walking through the fields. The voices grew closer. I got up, slipped into my clothes and stepped out into the cool, damp air. The women passed by the camp unseen, cloaked in darkness. Wrapping myself in a blanket, I walked down to the riverbank. The moon was still up, but a golden glow was spreading across the horizon. From the nearby village a lone dog howled. At the edge of the river, saddhus were doing puja, fashioning lingams from the muddy sand and anointing them with water. I sat down to watch another sunrise over the Ganga. Despite having spent an uncomfortable night in a straw hut, I felt immensely calm and ridiculously happy.

My good mood was soon taxed, however, by the overbearing scrutiny that dawn brought. A group of men sat around the doorway of our shelter, watching me thrash around under my blanket trying to divest some of the warm clothing I'd piled on earlier. Soon they were joined by three village women who followed me to the river, chattering like birds, and squatted on their haunches to peer at me washing my face and cleaning my teeth. They were quickly dispersed by the Bouncing Baba, who descended on them with wildly flapping hands, like some exotic bird. This was a Tuesday, his weekly day of silence, but he was managing to be as bossy as the night before. Through a combination of grunting and gesticulation, he led me to the camp kitchen, where he bade me sit on the sandy ground and thrust a lump of gur into my hand. Tackling this sweet, cloying stuff at seven in the morning was bad enough, but worse was to come. Over by the cooking fire, an old saddhu was peeling a heap of freshly boiled potatoes, while another was mashing them with his hands. The baba grabbed a peeled potato and gave it to me. At first I was relieved to exchange my gur for something more palatable, but I'd barely finished the first potato when another was passed over, and a pair of blazing eyes commanded me to eat it. Three potatoes later, in an attempt to fend off the tuber attack without upsetting anyone, I retrieved my lump of gur from the ground, picked off as much sand as I could and began nibbling on it. By now one of the old saddhus was bent over a large pot on the fire, stirring up a mixture of mashed potatoes and water and adding various brightly colored spices. Issuing thanks all around, I sidled over towards the door of the hut, but before I could reach it the baba handed me a bowl heaped with the potato sabzee and sprinkled with cardamom seeds. Then he dipped a metal beaker into a pail of water that had just been carried up from the river, handed it to me and, with his face six inches from mine, glared at me until I drank it all.

By eight the camp was bustling with activity. A line of singing women, perhaps the ones I'd heard hours before, marched through the camp carrying on their heads bundles of sugar cane and coconuts. Bejeweled ankles and toes flashed from beneath their saris, and glass bracelets jangled on their wrists. This was the day of the full moon, and they were on their way to the river to make a special puja to ask for the protection of their newly sown crops. Actors just up from bathing in the Ganga shivered around straw fires, putting their bare feet right into the flames and holding up sodden undershorts to dry. Musicians began warming up on their tablas and harmoniums. Villagers were setting up refreshment stalls selling bidis, sweets, pakora and guavas. Dag, Bapi and I had a quick conference. Staying to watch the play, which would doubtless be a protracted affair, would cause us to lose yet another day of paddling. We were about to reach a consensus decision to pack up and leave when the Bouncing Baba joined us and began scrawling Hindi words in the sand with his finger.

"He says we must stay until tomorrow," Bapi translated.

Regretfully, we told him this wasn't possible.

The baba's eyes blazed as he dashed off his next message.

"He says he will start the play immediately and that we can leave by noon."

Rather reluctantly, we settled down in front of the stage. For the next hour, however, we were the main entertainment, watched by an appreciative and ever-swelling audience. The actors and musicians busied about to no obvious effect, and the saddhus sat around our kayaks firing up one chillum after another. Sensing our restlessness, the Bouncing Baba set upon the troupe with a bamboo cane, thwacking its members into action. Eventually, eight men stood on stage in front of a backdrop depicting a room with an arched pink and green ceiling, orange and yellow striped pillars and a golden chandelier. Five of the men were dressed as women, but the effect of their makeup, jewelry and the false breasts straining at their saris was rather spoiled by their heavy wristwatches and their heels poking out of well-worn nylon socks. They launched into a sinuous dance which, after half an hour, proved to be only a preamble to the play. A new backdrop came down, and now the scene was of the Ganga flowing out of the Himalayas alongside a four-lane highway. Three of the actors came center stage and began to sing.

"This is Rama, his wife Sita and his brother Lakshmana," explained Bapi. "They are going into exile in the jungle, where Lakshmana will be cutting off the ears of the sister of Ravana, who in revenge for this will be carrying off Sita, so that Rama will be making an alliance with Sugriva, king of the monkeys, who will be sending Hanuman to help him, and Hanuman will be building a dam across the straits—"

"Stop!" I implored him. "You're going too fast, I'm lost. How do you know all this?"

"I learned the story when I was a child. And now it is a soap opera on the television."

By noon, the wind was blowing sand around the camp and whipping up lengths of orange cloth from the straw roofs where they'd been left to dry. Bapi had wandered off to share a chillum with the saddhus, and the play had ground to a halt. All the actors were now on stage, huddled behind a man in a dhoti and a jacket who was hectoring the audience to make donations to the theater troupe. As rupees were passed up, he announced the names of the donors and the exact amount of their donations. An hour later, with the play still no further forward and a sandstorm threatening, we decided that we would leave after all. Our announcement to this effect caused the baba to fly into a temper, and he scribbled furious messages into the sand: that our departure would once again disrupt the entire proceedings, that we should stay another night, and the next day as well. When we were adamant, he demanded that Dag and Bapi go on to the stage and explain to the crowd why we were leaving. Dag said a few words in English about our reasons for having to press on to Varanasi, then Bapi took the microphone to translate and launched into a long, rambling, marijuana-inspired speech. When the time came for us to say good-bye to the baba, he sat with his arm over his eyes, literally refusing to see us.

The scene of our departure was even more chaotic than our arrival the day before. The entire audience, the actors, the musicians and most of the saddhus came to see us off. Dag left me and Bapi standing knee-deep in the river, hanging on to our boats and submerged by people, while he sprinted up the hill to take a photo of the scene. Even when we paddled off, the crowd stayed with us, running along the banks and only gradually falling back and returning to the play.

Despite a stiff wind that whipped up clouds of stinging sand, it was a relief to be back on the Ganga and alone once more. Flocks of cranes and cormorants flapped up from the river, bright white and deep black against a gray landscape and sky. Sometimes people emerged from the sand clouds, like ghosts in a dream: a lunatic sitting on the bank gabbling to himself, a bare-chested Brahmin wearing the sacred thread across his torso, doing puja in celebration of the full moon. The sounds of drumming and singing drifted from nearby villages, but we paddled on until we were bathed in moonlight, and camped alone and undisturbed on a muddy bank.

15

Blessings and Bodies

While Dag still slept, I crawled out of the tent. In the dawn light the river looked like dull pewter, and tendrils of mist crept along its surface. Quickly, I undressed, and despite my only companions being two red-legged storks delicately stepping across a nearby sandbar, I wrapped myself in a length of cloth. I'd learned that in India people can materialize from nowhere, and to be found bathing naked in the Ganga would be an untenable transgression of holy law. As I waded into the sluggish water, the storks flapped their wings and skimmed away with long legs trailing behind them. Holding my nose, I immersed myself for three quick, cold dips, then struggled back to the bank. Bending to my small pile of clothes, I realized I was standing among cinders and brittle bone fragments. Nearby, a makeshift stretcher and a muddy shroud lay discarded.

After three weeks on the river, we'd grown used to seeing cremations in all their various stages. We'd seen naked corpses being ceremonially smeared with ghee, we'd seen a man carrying a lighted torch five times around the pyre on which his dead father lay, we'd seen people too poor to afford enough fuel simply pushing a half-burned body into the water. Later that day, as we paddled by the third cremation in as many hours, Dag and Bapi lapsed into black humor.

"Smells like chicken—must have been a skinny one."

"No, no, you are quite wrong, it is smelling exactly like roast beef This was a fatter person!"

As always, the mourners ran to the water's edge, beckoning to us. We didn't intend to stop. We wanted to reach Fatehgarh that day, and we had no clear idea of the distance we had to cover.

"You will get there by nightfall," a saddhu we'd met earlier had predicted.

"It's fifty kilometers away," a fisherman standing waist-deep in the river had told us. Now, the mourners had yet another estimate.

"Do sau kilomitar!" they cried. "Two hundred kilometers! Come and rest!"

We put our palms together in *namaskar* and carried on. After a few paddle strokes, I turned to wave at the men. They were shading their eyes with their hands to watch our departure. Seen through the flame-heated air, they appeared to shimmer, like ghostly creatures. The river took a wide bend, and suddenly the men were out of sight.

The next section of the river had a forsaken feeling to it. It made tortuous loops, a hot searing wind swept across the plain and the sky glared down. There was nothing to distract us from the monotony save sandbanks and skeletons. Once, we became stranded on a bank in the company of a full human skeleton, picked clean of flesh but with cloth still wrapped around its torso.

We'd already given up the idea of trying to reach Fatehgarh that day when we saw a red flag fluttering from a long pole, the sign of an encampment of saddhus. Drifting toward us on the wind were the rhythmic beating of a gong and the droning of a mantra: "Sita Ram Sita Ram Sita Ram Sita Ram . . ." A crowd of saddhus ran down to the riverbank and pulled our boats ashore. They had long matted hair and were ash-smeared and naked except for loincloths. Around their feet, scabby, dun-colored dogs barked, leaped and fought, raising clouds of sand. The saddhus told us they were camped here for the month of Magh with their 111-year-old guru, Moni Baba. Chattering excitedly, they led us to a large tent made of ragged canvas thrown over bamboo poles. Next to it, some women from the nearby village of Kadarga were sitting in the dirt making rotis and potato sabzee. They stopped working to stare at us, and the cloud of flies buzzing around them settled onto the dough, changing its pasty gray color to black.

Inside the tent, the ground was spread with dusty straw and the

air was thick with flies, but it was a welcome respite from the wind
and the blinding light outside. We were brought mugs of lukewarm tea that was the same muddy color as the river. Several saddhus crouched around to watch us drink it. Others peered
around the tent flap and through holes in the canvas. Despite my
strong suspicion that the water hadn't been boiled, I gulped it
down. The saddhus grinned in delight. The tent flap was thrown
back and a young saddhu came in with two plates heaped with
sabzee and rotis. Fleetingly, I remembered the fly-covered dough
outside, and then I pushed the thought aside.

"They are asking us to sleep tonight in this tent," said Bapi.

I looked doubtfully at the thick cloud of flies circling our
heads. The saddhus' eyes followed mine.

"They are telling," said Bapi, "that you must not worry about
these flies, because when darkness comes they will go home."

Bowls of warm buffalo milk and lumps of gur followed next. To
allay the arrival of yet more food, we requested an audience with
Moni Baba.

We were ushered to the doorway of a tiny tent. Two saddhus
knelt either side of a heap of blankets and began singing to it.
The heap stirred. A hand emerged. The blankets were thrown
back and a wizened old man sat up. His rheumy eyes were heavily lidded and his head was totally bald except for a few long
strands of fine hair sprouting from the crown. He was instantly
alert and listened carefully to the saddhus' explanation of who we
were and what we were doing. Then, as this was his weekly day of
silence, he reached for a chalkboard. While he scrawled some
Hindi script, I noticed how remarkably young his hands looked.
Bapi translated what he wrote.

"Moni Baba says that our yatra purifies the food we eat and the
water we drink."

With a measure of relief, I thought of the meal we'd just consumed.

"He says that we will reach Varanasi in safety, but the hardest
part of the journey is ahead. He says that we should sing *Rama
Sita.*"

The guru began clapping his hands together. Feeling rather
self-conscious, we chanted the mantra in time with him. The saddhus pressing around the tent joined in, the man beating the
gong fell into our rhythm, conches were blown, cymbals clashed

and soon the entire camp echoed with fervent singing. Despite the heat inside the tent, and the flies crawling over my face and arms, I felt myself slipping into a strange, hypnotic state, and I gazed in homage at the old man before me. Abruptly, he held up his hands for silence. All around the camp, the singing and music faded away. He closed his eyes, and his lips moved as if in prayer. There was a pregnant hush in and around the tent. Then the guru's heavy lids snapped open, and his eyes twinkled at Dag.

"Good day, sir!" he cried, and dissolved into helpless chuckling.

The saddhus gasped in alarm: the guru had broken his day of silence!

Moni Baba composed himself.

"Today I go to Varanasi," he solemnly pronounced. "Yesterday, I went to Varanasi. Tomorrow I shall go to Varanasi."

"He is practicing his English!" cried Bapi.

The guru sneezed.

"Rama!" yelled the saddhus in unison. "Sita Ram!" A fresh round of chanting and clapping ensued.

When darkness came, the flies did go home, forming a dense coating on the inside walls and ceiling of the tent. I lay in our sleeping bag, listening to the muttering of mantras all around the camp and wondering if Moni Baba had been right about the purification of our food. Since leaving Hardwar, every night I'd expected to wake up with the gut-wrenching pains that presage an attack of gastroenteritis. So far, though, I'd had the opposite problem: whether it was because of the starchy diet, or as a result of my inhibitions due to the lack of privacy and toilet paper, I was suffering, on the Ganges of all places, from constipation.

At six o'clock the flies woke and descended upon us, forcing us to flee the tent. All around the camp, saddhus were meditating, or doing puja at the water's edge, or hunkered around small fires. Moni Baba's appearance at eight drew them all together, and they greeted him with fervent delight, blowing on conches, banging on cymbals, gongs, drums and tin plates, and shouting out mantras. He shuffled along to a small platform shaded with yellow cloth, where he was lifted up to sit amid heaps of flowers, tin boxes filled with blessed sweets, pictures of Rama and holy books bound in red cloth. One by one the saddhus knelt before him to receive his blessing and accept a prasad of sweets. Then it was our turn. We strewed marigolds over his head and touched our foreheads to his feet. As he gave us prasad, he spoke in a childish, singsong voice.

Bapi's face broke into a huge grin. "Moni Baba is wanting to see your kayak!"

Helped by the saddhus, the guru inched his way to the river-bank. For several minutes he stood in silence, staring down at the red boat. When he finally spoke his words were greeted with gasps and squeals of surprise.

"He is wanting to ride in the boat!" cried Bapi.

"Rama Sita!" the saddhus shouted. "Sita Ram!"

I held the boat steady as the old man was lowered into the front cockpit. He pulled his shawl tightly around his shoulders, and held out one hand for his staff, which he laid across the deck. Dag got into the back of the kayak, tentatively pushed off from the bank and paddled the frail guru around in circles.

"Sita Ram, Sita Ram!" sang the saddhus, leaping about in pure joy and showering the boat with marigold heads.

"If you insist on these tearful leave-takings, you'd better learn how to blow your nose the Indian way," said Dag as we paddled away from the camp.

Overcome by the exuberant faith of the saddhus, and by their open-hearted acceptance of us, I was openly weeping. By the time I managed to stop the flood of tears, their chanting had faded out of earshot, and the marigold heads on the kayak deck were withering in the sun.

The river still lazily wound about, and despite long days of pad-dling we seemed to get no closer to Fatehgarh. But there was a change of atmosphere along the riverbanks. The curiosity of the farmers we met along the way was tinged with suspicion and resentment, and the warnings of dacoits steadily increased.

"There are jungle people around here," the farmers said. "You must not camp alone."

We finally reached the outskirts of Fatehgarh on a bright and sunny morning. Women in vivid saris worked in fields of pump-kins and mustard, and dhobi wallahs stood in the river, wrestling with huge lengths of material which stained the water with red and purple dyes. All over the bank, shirts, saris and bolts of cot-ton were spread out to dry in the afternoon sun. Burros lay in the dirt, curled up and sleeping like dogs.

"To your left," said Dag.

I looked, and wished I hadn't. A few feet away from us, the corpse of a young man floated on its side in a fetal position. The bloated skin was a sickly yellow color, and part of the face was eaten away. During four weeks on the Ganges, my stomach had hardened up enough to withstand fly-infested food and water straight from the river, but this was simply too much for it.

"Are you OK?" asked Dag, when I stopped retching. "Because there's another one up ahead."

During the next twenty minutes, we paddled past a dozen more bodies. The fresher ones were still wrapped in cloth which ballooned up above the surface of the water. From a distance, they could have been mistaken for discarded pillowcases, were it not for the crows and vultures which flapped down to peck at them and the dogs which swam out for a meal. One of the bodies was tragically comical, floating face down with only the buttocks showing above the water. Another lay trapped on a sandbank, its ribcage exposed and pieces of its flesh fluttering in the current. But worst of all was the corpse which had become completely submerged save for the feet: toes splayed, skin mottled and shrunken, and murky water concealing the horror below. This was the stuff of nightmares.

It was enough for one day. We went ashore at the ghats of a small temple, and the pujari hurried down to meet us.

"You are making a thesis about this river?" he shouted, standing a mere two feet away.

"Yes, we're collecting material for a book," I replied.

"Very good! Very good! You are a poet?"

I told him I wasn't, and he shook his head as if in consolation.

"Oh dear. I am very sorry. Here in India, we like poets very much. What is the difference between India and your country?"

A corpse floated by; downstream, dogs fought over another that lay rotting on the bank.

"India is spiritual," I said. "My country is materialistic."

"Ah, yes," he responded. "I have been hearing this before. Where is God?"

"God is everywhere," I replied.

"It is true!" he cried, clapping his hands. "Perhaps your husband is Lord Rama and you are his wife, Sita! So we treat you as our gods! You must sleep here tonight! There are many robbers close by but have no fear, we will be guarding you."

Leaving the kayaks in his care, we walked into Fatehgarh. As we stopped off at street stalls to buy fruit, tea and rice, people pressed in at our backs and elbows, making it difficult for us to move. By the time we arrived at the post office, from where I wanted to place a call to my mother, the crowd had grown and practically filled the small room, where an ill-tempered clerk sat behind a desk.

"What is the code number for England?" I asked him.

Impatiently, he paged through a battered, torn telephone directory.

"You've gone past it," I told him.

He slammed the book shut. "The international section is missing!" he shouted. "You must call from Varanasi!"

"I won't be there for two weeks," I protested. "Can't you call the operator?"

"The operator has gone!" he shouted.

"It's very important that I talk to my mother," I coaxed. "Please show me the directory."

Reluctantly, he handed it over. Within seconds, I had located the international section and the country code for England. The clerk passed me an ancient black telephone, and I dialed my mother's number. There were whooshing and fizzing noises on the line, as if I was trying to connect with outer space, then a clear ringing began. On either side of me were men with their faces about three inches away from mine, and their eyes popping with curiosity.

"Hello, Mum," I said, when she answered. "I'm calling from a small town along the Ganges."

"She is calling her mother," announced the clerk to the crowd. "Her mother is living in England. She is happy to be hearing from her daughter."

"How are you?" asked my mother. "What on earth is it like over there?"

"We're both really healthy," I said. "And it's incredible here, it's heartbreaking, inspiring, everything you can and can't imagine."

Frowning, the clerk scratched his head. "She is telling her mother how is the weather!" he triumphantly announced to the expectant crowd.

"What are you laughing about?" asked my mother.

16

A Change in Atmosphere

According to the pujari in Fatehgarh, the corpses in the river were the remains of people stricken by infectious disease, or whose families could not afford the fuel for a pyre, or who had died unmarried. This last fact upset Bapi, and he fretted about it all day.

"I must discuss it with my parents!" he repeatedly cried. "I do not want to be ending up in the river!"

Neither did we. Traveling so slowly and so visibly, with only nylon walls to protect us at night, we were feeling increasingly vulnerable. The closer we got to the industrial city of Kanpur, the dirtier the river became and the more disquieting the atmosphere along its banks. At Singrampurghat, the faded paintings of peacocks and snakes on the arches of an old temple had Hindi graffiti scrawled over them, and there were little piles of human feces up and down the stone steps. A few yards from where a corpse floated on its back, several men were standing on the shore, drying themselves after a ritual bath. Their rifles lay around their feet, and as we paddled by one man reached for his weapon and sprinkled it with a libation of river water.

As the afternoon wore on we began moving through a predominantly Muslim area. People stared suspiciously at us from villages cut into the steep rock escarpments on the permanent bank. When we asked if they knew where we could find shelter for the night they shrugged and shook their heads. We paddled close to Bapi, who was visibly tense. The river looped away from the permanent bank and out into the plain, where once more it began dividing up into a maze of small channels. There was no way of knowing which one carried the main flow, so we chose at random. Half a mile on, the water in our channel petered out, and we were stuck. Children from the last village had followed us thus far, and now, as the sun slipped down behind the horizon, they ran back home.

"No doubt," commented Dag, "to tell their fathers about the three sitting ducks on the river."

"I am not feeling at all happy about camping here," said Bapi. "Perhaps we will be waking up with our throats slit."

For half an hour we heaved our boats through the trickle of water, until finally we met up again with the main channel. A short distance downstream, on the far bank, we saw the glow of a fire.

"These people could be fishermen or dacoits," said Bapi. "I will go ahead and talk to them."

Slowly, we paddled behind him, straining our eyes to see through the fast-descending gloom to the small encampment. There was one large shelter set up, made from a tarpaulin slung across bamboo poles sticking out of the sand. Large, flat baskets were scattered over the shore, and as we drew nearer we passed a man standing waist-deep in water and using one of these baskets to scoop up tiny silvery fish.

"Come on, come on!" shouted Bapi. "It is safe!"

Twenty-five fishermen were camped at that desolate spot, waiting for a contractor to arrive and collect their catch. They were all armed with large rifles which they casually slung over their shoulders. They told us we were lucky to have come across this encampment, as there were many dacoits about.

"At first they were thinking we were dacoits," said Bapi. "They could not understand what it is we are doing here, so I told them Maria is a writer with a special interest in Hindustani fishermen."

Twenty-five pairs of eyes watched us unpack and set up our tent. When I lifted Dag's telescopic camera tripod from the kayak, the eyes narrowed.

"They are asking if it is a gun," said Bapi. "So I am telling them, 'What do you think? These people are well prepared.'"

They must also have wondered why the writer with a special interested in Hindustani fishermen crawled away into her tent without asking anyone a single question. I was too exhausted to eat, and rather than sit around the fire considering our situation—out in the middle of the Gangetic Plain with twenty-five heavily armed strangers—I preferred to escape into sleep.

When I unzipped the tent door at six o'clock next morning, twenty-five pairs of eyes were still focused on me. Most of the fishermen lay under the tarpaulin, wrapped in dirty blankets and cotton quilts and with their guns at their sides. Some of them were already up and were sitting round the fire sharing a chillum. I walked away from the camp to find a private spot for my morning ablutions. But the river was so slimy and so stinking of rotting fish that I couldn't face washing in it. I felt absolutely wretched. My hair, skin and nails were grimy, I had fungus growing on various parts of my body, and my few articles of clothing, which I was thoroughly sick of wearing, were in dire need of a wash. I'd just spent the night in bandit country, and, to cap it all, in two days' time I was going to turn forty. Glumly I returned to the tent. Bapi was sitting outside it, and he made a valiant attempt to cheer me up.

"Maria, it is a great achievement," he said, in the respectful tone he'd adopted since discovering my age, "for a woman as old as you to go on such a journey!"

"And just think," added Dag, "you can claim to be the first woman to turn forty while kayaking down the Ganges!"

It was little consolation. Over the next few hours of paddling I hardly noticed a pale golden light spreading across the plain, the sky fading from gray into blue, the vultures fighting over a washed-up corpse. I'd escaped to London, where, after having my hair washed and cut, and spending a considerable amount of money on clothes, I was walking through pale winter sunshine towards a Covent Garden restaurant, on my way to a long, leisurely and utterly civilized birthday lunch.

"*Ana! Ana!* Come! Come!"

The shouts interrupted me just as I was about to look over the wine list.

"Ana!"

We had taken the left channel around a large sand island and were paddling quite close to the far riverbank. The man shouting to us was striding along the shore of the island, a hundred yards away, and clutching a rifle. Sensing that this was no friendly farmer wanting us to stop for a chat, without a word to each other

Dag and I picked up speed until water flew from the end of our paddles.

"Ana!" yelled the man. "Ana!"

He lifted his rifle and leveled it at us.

"Jesus!"

"Move it!" barked Dag, and I paddled as if my life depended on it, which it probably did. The man broke into a run, shouting and waving his gun. At the end of the sand island he gave up the chase, but we maintained our speed up for another half a mile, until we saw a temple on the shore and a red flag fluttering from a pole. When we pulled ashore, I began trembling uncontrollably.

"I'm pretty sure we were out of his accurate range," said Dag tersely, "but I hope Bapi's OK."

Ten minutes later we saw the flash of Bapi's paddles in the sunlight.

"Did that bloody madman chase you, too?" he cried as the prow of his boat hit the shore.

A saddhu wearing a large digital wristwatch had come down from the temple to greet us, and now he turned to Bapi with a torrent of Hindi. Bapi listened seriously, waggling his head and assenting with "Acchha, acchha."

"He is insisting we must not carry on with our journey. He is saying that between here and Allahabad is a most dangerous place, the dacoits have rifles and hand grenades. He is telling us it is not safe for us to camp by this temple, but that a little way down the river there is a house where we can rest in peace."

Dilip Saxena's house stood on a high bank overlooking the Ganges. It was an old colonial building once owned by the British Army, now falling into disrepair amid dusty, windswept gardens. The rooms were cool and shuttered, with thick stone walls, flagged floors and an odd assortment of Indian and British furniture. Dilip received us with a disinterested air, but was kind nonetheless, offering us shelter for the night and, if we wished it, transportation by pony trap to the bus station the next day.

Sitting in the sunshine on a charpoi, Dag, Bapi and I discussed what to do. The two men agreed that we should avoid the stretch of river infamous for dacoits, and go by road to Allahabad. I, surprising even myself, argued vehemently for carrying on by kayak. I felt inextricably linked to the Ganga, as if I'd made her a promise that I could not break. Despite its hardships, and now its dangers, the river gave me a sense of contentment and peace which I couldn't bear to be dragged away from.

"We must carry on," I said. "We're on a pilgrimage, a stream of grace."

Dag rolled his eyes. "Tell that to the dacoits when they're at the other end of a gun."

"We can stick close to Bapi," I insisted, "and we can make sure we're off the river and in a village each day by early afternoon."

"Maria, what if we are finding no village?" asked Bapi. "Really, I do not want us to be camping alone in this area. There are too many terrible stories about."

"By road it's about a hundred and twenty-five miles from here to Allahabad," added Dag, "and two, maybe three times as much by river. If we only paddled in the mornings, it would take us a week to cover that distance, and that wouldn't give us time to reach Varanasi by the second week of March."

I was outvoted: we were to go by bus to Allahabad. While Dag and Bapi took our kayak apart, I sulkily went for a wash. Dilip's wife carried a bucket of warm water into a room off the courtyard. In one corner there was a small drain, and in the other a manger filled with straw. While I gave myself a much-needed scrub, a cow wearing a red scarf round its neck plaintively mooed outside the door, obviously put out that I had disrupted its feeding time.

That night, as if he'd decided that the journey was practically over, Bapi began reminiscing about the experiences we'd shared.

"When we arrived in Gessapur," he said, "some of the villagers were opposed to us staying there."

Shocked, Dag and I stared at him.

"Really, Bapi? Why?"

"They said it was because you were foreigners, and also so untidy."

I thought back to the women peeling off my dusty clothes, and my toes curled with embarrassment.

"Why didn't you tell us?"

"There was no point. It was sorted out."

I thought for a moment. "What else didn't you tell us, Bapi?"

"Oh, this and that," he said. "Always the people were telling me what their caste was and asking me about yours."

"Why didn't you translate this?"

"Caste is a bad system. I didn't wish to speak of it, it was too embarrassing."

Anger bubbled up inside me. "What do you mean, you didn't wish to speak of it? You were supposed to be interpreting, but you were censoring what was being said!"

"Maria, that's not fair," interjected Dag. "You don't speak a second language, so you've no idea of how difficult translation is. This is Bapi's first shot at it and he's been doing well."

"Really, Maria, I have been trying my best," said Bapi, his face a picture of hurt. "I have been telling you what I thought was useful."

Although remorseful, I was still smarting about the decision to pull off the river, and I went to sleep without apologizing.

For once, Bapi was the first up next morning.

"You hurt his feelings," Dag told me as we stepped from the dark room into warm sunshine.

Dilip's servant, an old man with bandy legs, fussed around us, bringing chai and biscuits, and then watched awestruck as I prepared to insert my contact lenses. It occurred to me, as I set out the bottles of solution and washed my hands in a small bowl of water, that to him this must have seemed like some Westernized form of puja.

"Bapi kahan hai?" I asked him. "Where's Bapi?"

He pointed towards the river. "Ghat," he said.

"Let's go and find him," I suggested to Dag. He picked up his yellow camera case and followed me down the bank.

The ghat was a small sandy beach, not more than fifty feet long. At one end a pujari sat next to a tray of offerings to sell to people who came from the nearby village for morning puja. At the other end Bapi stood stock still, facing the river. I walked over to him, and was about to touch his arm and offer my apologies when I saw what he gazing at. At the water's edge was the body of a young girl, maybe five years old. Her black, shoulder-length hair was caked with mud. She lay on her back, with one arm thrown over her face as if to shield her eyes from the sun, or from the horror that had befallen her. A dog was chewing on one of her legs; it had already consumed her foot and was halfway up her calf. I froze, and the sounds of the sun-dappled morning seemed to sharpen—the catlike cries of a peacock, the chirping of sparrows, the tearing of flesh, the crunching of bone. Shaking its head hard, the dog flipped the girl over, and she landed on the sand with a dull thump. I turned away and put hands over my ears, but the sight and sounds were imprinted on my memory.

"She was thrown in the river last night," said Bapi quietly. "The pujari pulled her out an hour ago."

"Why didn't he leave her in there?" I whispered.

"The river is so low and sluggish, she would pollute this place where people are bathing. Really, it is better that the dogs are getting her."

It was an inauspicious start to the day, which an eight-hour bus journey along the Grand Trunk Road did little to improve. The bus careered through small towns, constantly swerving around cows and out of the path of oncoming traffic. Within the first half-hour we drove past the smoldering remains of two grisly vehicle crashes, making me consider that perhaps we would have been safer on the river after all.

Two brave tricycle wallahs insisted they could transport us and our boats on their gaudily painted vehicles from the bus station in Allahabad's old town to a hotel called the Tourist Bungalow. We sat atop our two bags, while Bapi perched on the back of the other tiny carrier, clinging to his boat, which stuck nine feet into the air like a giant arrow.

As we approached the Tourist Bungalow, Dag nudged me.

"Over there!" he shouted, pointing to a man and woman walking along the road. Blond, dressed in scarlet and carrying rucksacks, they were the first Westerners we'd seen for over a month.

"Aren't they strange?" he mused, craning his neck for a better view. "No wonder everyone's staring at them."

As this was the eve of my birthday, Dag decided to treat me to a posh meal, and the receptionist of the Tourist Bungalow recommended the Tandoor Restaurant. On the way there we passed a row of food stalls illuminated by mercury lamps, where local people sat on wooden benches eating simple curries with rotis straight from clay ovens.

"Let's go to one of these instead," I suggested.

I was still attached to the simplicity of our life on the river, and not really ready to face a sophisticated restaurant. But Dag insisted that I deserved something special. The Tandoor was full of wealthy Indians, the men in well-tailored suits, the women garbed in gorgeous silk saris and lots of gold jewelry. Since leaving Hardwar, we'd eaten only vegetarian food. Not wanting to break this aspect of our "stream of grace," I ordered a humble dish of dhal and peas. Dag, however, opted for lamb curry and Bapi for chicken. The rotis were served in filigreed silver baskets, and we toasted my birthday with ice cold Guru beer.

"Wouldn't it be a joke if we got sick in a place like this?" quipped Dag.

"You deserve to," I teased him, "for eating meat along the holy river."

In the middle of the night he woke up groaning and clutching his stomach. Early on the morning of my fortieth birthday I lay in bed helplessly listening to him in the adjoining bathroom, suffering a violent attack of gastroenteritis.

For the next twenty-four hours Dag's temperature steadily rose, and when he wasn't uttering wretched sounds in the bathroom he was pacing around, breathing through his pain like a woman in labor. It was obvious that we wouldn't be leaving Allahabad in a hurry, and that evening the decision was made that Bapi should return to New Delhi. He was anxious about some pressing work and family commitments, while Dag and I had begun to feel that we should experience this last part of our trip along the Ganga without Bapi as a buffer. We knew we were going to miss him, though, and we sadly waved good-bye as a rickshaw wallah pedaled him out of the Tourist Bungalow compound and back to the bus station.

Two days later we set off early in the morning to rejoin the river, looking far more respectable than when we'd left it. I'd given our clothes to the hotel's dhobi wallah, apologizing for their appalling state. They were returned missing several buttons and, in the case of our socks and thermal underwear, several sizes bigger than before, but startlingly clean.

There are seven sacred rivers in India, and Allahabad is situated at the convergence of three of them, the Ganga, the Yamuna and the invisible Saraswati. We launched the kayak on the Yamuna and floated toward the *sangam,* the meeting-point of the three rivers. The morning was warm, and in the bright sunlight the deep, slow-moving waters of the Yamuna were a sparkling greeny-blue. Wooden pilgrim boats rowed by us, going upstream from the sangam, their canopies spread with the drying clothes of the bathers inside. We passed beneath the massive sixteenth-century fort of Akbar, built of roughly cut stones which, from our perspective, each looked to be the size of a house. Beyond the fort, on the same side of the river, was a large promontory of sand almost obscured by the colorful throng of people swarming across it. Winding through the crowds were long processions led by men beating on drums, blowing on discordant pipes and holding aloft yellow and orange flags. Had it not been for the bicycles and the tour buses inching through the confusion, it could have been a medieval scene. Everyone was focused on a point where hundreds of stalls were set up on the shore, where the water was erupting with the splashing of innumerable bathers, where a thick swarm of boats bobbed about, where incense hung thickly in the air and where we finally put down our paddles and simply floated: the point where the clear Yamuna met and was swallowed up by the muddy Ganga. The actual confluence was surprisingly obvious, like an undulating line drawn between the two rivers. We turned the boat so that our bow faced along it. For several seconds we were held in limbo, gazing at the garlands of marigolds strewn across the water. Suddenly, the Ganga drew us to her, and a pod of dolphins surfaced around us as if in welcome. It was with a strong sense of homecoming that we turned the kayak and headed downstream.

On the edge of Manaiya village, we cooked dhal over our stove and ate it watching a hazy mauve sunset beyond the deep golds and greens of the wheat fields. Crickets whirred, toads croaked, jackals yelped and fruit bats rustled in the branches above us. Music and singing drifted from the temple, growing louder and softer as the wind shifted. A man called Dukhi, who was most distressed by us preparing our own food, insisted that we visit his home. Although Manaiya had only 300 inhabitants and no running water, it was serviced by electricity. In a house built of mud bricks with a terra-cotta tiled roof, we watched a cricket match played in Australia between India and Pakistan, and ate rice sweetened with coconut chips and raisins.

"We are poor," said Dukhi. "You are rich. We are happy that you accept our simple food."

One of the neighbors murmured something to Dukhi.

"He is asking what is your caste," he translated.

"What is yours?" we inquired.

"We are Sudras, of the boatman caste."

"We are also boatman caste," said Dag, and this was greeted with delight.

Someone had strung a light bulb from the nearest house and attached it to a bamboo pole next to our tent. As we prepared for bed, elongated shadows of the people hanging around outside were thrown across the nylon walls. At first these people were quiet, listening to the alien sounds emanating from inside the tent—zips closing, an air mattress inflating, Velcro strips coming apart, nylon rustling. Once we'd settled down, it was our turn to listen—to hawking and spitting, to puzzled conversations in Hindi about our water filter hanging from the tent door, to yelping dogs being thwacked. Then we heard something heavy being dragged towards us, and Dukhi shooing everyone away.

"Mr. Dag!" he called. "Do not be fearing! I will be guarding you!"

With that, he stretched out on the charpoi he'd brought from his house, fell asleep and kept us awake all night with his snoring.

At dawn I crept past him and went down to the field. From the private place I found behind a row of corn that shivered in the breeze, I watched an old man coming up from the riverbank. He wore a dhoti and kurta, a pink scarf wrapped around his bald head and a blanket. He was carrying a staff and a canister of water, and he prayed aloud as he walked up through the fields. Beyond him, the flood plain was bathed in an amber light, and bronze rays were fanning across the sky. The path took the man close by my hiding place. His mumbling faded away, but I stayed where I was, staring at the space he had passed through, not wanting to disturb the dreamlike quality of these moments, suddenly aware that our time on the Ganga was soon to be over.

Fed by tributaries, the river became deep and fast-flowing. It was also busier. Camel trains plodded along the banks, carrying sand being dredged up with buckets from the riverbed. Fishermen plodded upstream like Volga slaves, hauling their boats by long ropes attached to the masts. Others relaxed on bedrolls inside the domed canopies of boats, while their cantilevered nets hung in the water. We passed electricity pylons, fortlike pump houses, and newly built ghats with concrete steps, and I began to long for the isolation of the upper part of the river, and the sense of timelessness we'd experienced there.

Laxagir village, set on a high cliff above the flood plain, had brick houses with television aerials on the tiled roofs and shiny tractors parked on the dirt road. We were invited to spend the night at Baba Ram Das's small ashram, a dusty, untidy place with a jumble of bikes leaning against the temple wall. Baba Ram Das was an obese, fierce-looking character with gray matted hair falling to his waist. When we were ushered through a rusty iron gate into the leaf-strewn courtyard, he was lying on a charpoi beneath a veranda, having his feet massaged by a young *sannyasin*. Propping himself on one elbow, the baba told us we could stay, then ordered his followers to clean the place up. His followers didn't take kindly to this, or to us. They scurried around, sweeping the floor, shouting at the children hanging around the gate and giving us resentful glances. We were shown into our room for the night. It had a door made of corrugated iron, sacking spread over the floor, a wooden table, and a few bricks knocked out of one wall to form a window. I peered outside. The sun was a pale, yellowish-white dish, almost indistinguishable in a sky and above a landscape of identical hues.

At 5:00 A.M. the sounds of morning puja blared out from the speakers hanging up close to our cell. I had just scrambled out of bed and was half dressed when the door was flung open, and one of the bad-tempered sannyasins marched in and set down two beakers of tea on the table. I sat in the doorway to drink mine. A small village girl crept up to me, stared for a long time at my bare feet and then, mistaking my sunburn lines for dirt, began vigorously rubbing them with a moistened finger. Taking the hint, I persuaded Dag to come down to the river with me to wash. We'd already waded in up to our waists by the time we noticed a pair of buttocks floating nearby.

"That one followed us from Fatehgarh," joked Dag.

Beating a fast retreat, we adjourned to one of the village chai stalls, and sat in the warm morning sunshine, contentedly chatting to the villagers who gathered around. A policeman joined us, carelessly laying his rifle on the wooden bench.

"What is in the yellow box?" he asked.

"Cameras," Dag replied.

"Show me."

It was more of an order than a request. People pressed around as Dag opened the box, and sharp intakes of breath greeted the sight of a camera body and three lenses. I felt horribly embarrassed by this blatant show of our wealth, and the policeman's resentful expression unnerved me. Suddenly, I was anxious to get away from Laxagir, to be back on the Ganga and simply moving along with its flow.

"Let's make a move," I said to Dag, "before it gets too hot."

In the ashram, we hurriedly packed up. While Dag and a couple of sannyasins carried the boat to the water, I sorted out the rest of our gear. Catching sight of the baba in the courtyard, I popped out to give him a donation for the ashram. I was away from the room for perhaps three minutes, and returned to it at the same time as Dag.

"The door's closed," I said.

"So?"

"I'm sure I left it open."

We were gathering up the last of our belongings when Dag noticed a pair of white, upturned soles beneath the bed.

"There's a kid in here!" he cried, hauling out a small, skinny boy dressed in ripped shorts and shirt. "What the hell are you doing? Get lost!"

The boy was about to flee when the policemen we'd had tea with appeared in the doorway. He pushed the cowering boy into the corner and began poking him hard in the chest.

"What have you got?" he demanded. "Show me!"

It was only then that we realized the boy was clutching something in his trembling arms. *"Amrud, amrud,"* he whimpered. "Guavas, guavas."

"Show me!" the policeman shouted, but the boy held the bundle still tighter to his bony frame.

Still we didn't suspect the child of anything, not until the policeman yanked the bundle from him and unwrapped the filthy rags to reveal one of Dag's cameras.

"Holy smokes!" cried Dag, whirling round to the camera case he'd left lying on the table, which the child had carefully closed up again to cover the traces of his theft.

The policeman laid into the boy, slapping him hard on the head. When Dag tried to intervene, he grabbed the child by the hair and forced him to his knees.

"Beat him, sir! Beat him!"

There was nothing to be done but leave quickly. We hurried

down the bank, away from the thumps and yowls, sharing the same suspicious thought about the policeman.

The river was now a quarter of a mile wide, and we had a wind from behind that filled our sail and pushed us along at a fast clip. The banks rose into fluted sandstone cliffs with dramatic rock pillars and steep manmade stairways zigzagging down to the water. Ferries were being rowed across the river, and their passengers waved to us, once laughing uproariously when a gust of wind caught our sail and nearly tipped us. In terms of speed and distance covered, this was the most successful day we'd had during our five weeks on the river. Towards late afternoon we arrived at Mirzapur, a city literally crumbling into the Ganges. For two kilometers, the bank was lined with once grand temples and ashrams which were now dank and decaying. We pulled up at a ghat, and while Dag went to see if we could find accommodation in the ashram above it, I held on to the kayak, trying to ignore the raw, stinking sewage pouring from a pipe a few feet away. A wretched, filthy saddhu shuffled up to me, babbling and staring into my face. Teenage boys jeered at me, women collecting water not two feet from the sewer pipe gave me spiteful looks. Dag returned from the ashram, pursued by a raving madman in thick makeup who grabbed at his thighs and tried to pull down his shorts. We hurried on, but each place we stopped at was worse than the last: a ghat covered with mud and excrement, a dilapidated temple infested with rats, streets that were even dirtier and more foreboding than the riverfront. As the evening closed in, we paddled for a mile beyond the outskirts of the town. Seeing a fisherman casting his net, we headed over to him to ask advice. When he looked up, his face filled with terror and he scuttled fearfully to the far end of his boat.

"Jana! Jana!" he shouted. "Go away!"

Shortly afterwards, and to our great relief, a house with a red flag fluttering from it came into sight. We pulled ashore at the landing-point for a ferry, where a crowd of people were waiting for a ride across to the opposite bank. One of them ran up to the house for us, and returned with a young, stern-faced Brahmin.

"We are seeking a safe place to spend the night," we told him.

"You cannot stay here," he said.

"May we ask the baba?"

"It is not possible. You are not welcome. You must go away."

By now the ferry had arrived, and people were clambering aboard. The ferryman, who looked a fairly decent sort, called out *"Tahum jao sakte ho mera gaon!"* "You can go to my village!"

We looked to where he was pointing. Although there were no houses in sight, smoke and the glow of electric light rose above the trees. We thanked him, but a woman leaned down from the ferry, hanging over the side so far that her face almost touched mine.

"Khatara!" she hissed. *"Khatara!"* "Danger."

By now it was past six o'clock and almost dark. There was only one option left: to spend the night in the kayak, out on the river, and to paddle until dawn.

Luckily, the moon was waning and we were cloaked in darkness. From the villages along the shore we heard coughing, chanting, drumming, the wailing of babies—sounds once comfortingly familiar, now made sinister by the night and our vulnerability. Lights twinkled through trees, and sometimes there was the silhouette of a person, standing and perhaps wondering what the dogs had sensed to make them bark so furiously. We crept along like thieves, whispering to each other. Our quiet progress startled birds, which flapped up from the surface of the water right in front of the kayak, startling us in turn. Once we heard the mumbling of a mantra; a man was on the bank, hauling upstream a boat that came so close to us we could reach out and touch its gunnels. Sometimes, when the river divided around sand islands, we found ourselves in narrow channels, only feet away from camps of fishermen who huddled by fires, laughing coarsely. Fearing they might hear us, mistake us for dacoits and take a pot shot, we floated by with our breath held and our paddles out of the water. My other fear, irrational though it was, concerned the corpses. I dreaded bumping into one, and when we ran aground, as we did several times during that long night, before pushing off I tentatively poked around with my paddle, hoping that it wouldn't hit a rib cage or a face.

The tension was constant. It stiffened our necks and backs, it exhausted us to the point where we were wondered if the dolphins blowing around us were real or a hallucination. By 4:00 a.m. our nerves were frayed, we were cold and wretched and fed up with this river, with India, with kayaking. At 4:30, the lights of Chunar Fort appeared, glimmering like a specter almost 200 feet above the river. Floating in a back eddy, we waited for dawn, then went ashore on a sandbank below the impressive walls of the ancient fort. Wrapped in our blankets, we hunkered down by the water's edge. A lone fisherman poled by in his boat, looking as tired as we felt, but full of merry greetings. Like us, he seemed relieved that the long night was over.

Varanasi, our final destination, was now about thirty miles away. As we sat below Chunar Fort, breakfasting on water and raisins, Dag suggested doing one final push and ending the journey by nightfall. This filled me with conflicting feelings. Five weeks on the Ganga had left me physically, mentally and emotionally exhausted; my mind was crammed with its images and confusions, and the idea of any more floating corpses, muddy campsites or curious crowds of onlookers was simply unbearable. And yet, increasingly I was filled with dread at the thought of leaving the river. For years I had wanted to see the ancient city of Varanasi: now it was a place I was loath to reach.

17

Light Years Away

For two hours we drifted downstream. Ahead, the patchwork sails of fishing boats billowed in the wind, and on the left bank a host of red flags fluttered from a sandstone bluff.

"I don't want to stop," warned Dag.

Beneath the flags the shore was awash with color, as if a carpet of butterflies had settled on it. As we drew closer we saw a narrow ghat packed with people, who were spilling over into the river. Above them, on the steep bank, rows of pilgrims' huts were hung with lengths of brilliantly colored material, and flower sellers' baskets were heaped with red and orange blooms. The flags were flying from a yellow temple on the top of the bluff, and mud-colored buildings huddled at its base.

"Let's go and have a look," I coaxed.

"I can't stand another village," Dag insisted. "No more questions, no more staring, I've absolutely had it."

"Just for a minute," I persisted. "You stay in the boat, I'll go and buy some chai and samosas."

His resolve softened by the idea of hot tea and fresh food, Dag turned the rudder and we paddled up to the shore, a little way from the ghat. As I hopped out of the boat, a diminutive young man hurried over to me.

"What do you want?" he shouted. "How can I help you?"

"I want to buy some food," I told him.

"Come with me! I am Sudraj! This village is Sultanpur! What is your name? Maureeya? Nice name! Come on!"

I followed him up the steps and into a winding, bricked lane. Red dust motes danced in the sunlight shafting between softly contoured buildings. Long-eared goats wandered about, women carrying baskets of steaming dung on their heads sashayed by, pilgrims made their way to the river, singing as they went. Vendors called cheerfully to me from behind their stalls, where the red and orange sindoor powder used for tikkas had been heaped into perfect little pyramids.

"Here, Maureeya!" cried Sudraj. "Chai! Chai!"

The owner of the chai shop was hunkered on top of his adobe oven, frying pakora over the open fire and swatting away flies. He had a bull-like neck, a downturned betel-stained mouth and wild, staring eyes. Brusquely, he thrust a beaker of tea into my hands, then wrapped up several pakoras in a banana leaf for me. When I tried to pay him he waved away the money.

"He says it is a gift," said Sudraj.

On the riverbank, Dag was surrounded by men who were incredulous to hear that not only had we come all the way from Hardwar, but that we'd just paddled through the night from Mirzapur.

"Go and have a quick look around the village," I urged him.

He returned elated. "I take everything back," he said.

We asked the men if there was a place in Sultanpur where we could camp for the night.

"Acchha! Acchha!" they cried delightedly, and pointed up to where the red flags fluttered against the solid blue of the sky.

Thinking back to my Catholic days, I tried to imagine how I would have reacted to a pair scruffy foreigners camped in the church vestibule. It's doubtful that I'd have been quite as magnanimous as the pilgrims who arrived to worship Goddess Sitala and found our kayak and tent parked in a corner of the temple courtyard. They came all day in a steady stream, laden with offerings. They rang a brass bell hanging from the door of the shrine to announce their presence to the goddess, touched blessed sweets to her mouth, lay money at her feet, garlanded her and sprinkled her with coconut milk. Meanwhile, their children played in the courtyard, wriggling over the dusty stone slabs in a game of "snake" or chasing each other round and round our tent. Things got rather hectic during the noontime puja. Clamorous bells were rung and the little courtyard heaved with people pushing and shoving to get close to the shrine. The pujaris waved lights and incense around Sitala's small, gold-plated face, and when one of them emerged holding a bowl of burning camphor, there was a mad scramble as everyone reached forward to run their hands through the anointing flame. Another scrum ensued when the second pujari began handing out a prasad of blessed sweets. In the midst of this frenzy was the temple goat, happily gobbling up dropped sweets and tearing chunks off peoples' marigold garlands when they weren't looking.

The goat was a large bearded male, Billy Goat Gruff in the flesh, but Indianized with sandalwood paste smeared on his forehead. The pilgrims thoroughly spoiled him, reverently feeding him with coconuts, sweets and flowers. Our arrival left him deeply disgruntled. As soon as the kayak was set down, the prow sticking into what we later discovered was one of his favorite sleeping corners, he began determinedly nibbling on it. And to show his disgust of our tent, he repeatedly head butted it and left liberal amounts of his droppings around the door.

When the noon puja was over and things quieted down, I leaned on the wall of the small courtyard and gazed over the Gangetic Plain. After weeks on the river, it was dizzying to suddenly be high above it and have a bird's-eye view of the land we had journeyed across. Water and sand merged into each other, gray on white, to form an empty landscape that teemed with vivid life. I thought about all the paradoxes: the monsoons which swept away homes and laid down fertile soil, the compelling beauty of the poorest villages, the rotting corpses in a river said to have the power of physical and spiritual purification. I remembered the ministry official in New Delhi who had declared us potty for wanting to embark on this journey. I was glad we'd ignored his advice to reconsider our plans. It was a journey that had turned me inside out, challenged every one of my values, and made me question how, or why, I would ever return to the safe world, so bland and pale in comparison to this one, that I'd so long and so smugly inhabited.

My thoughts were abruptly interrupted by Sudraj.

"Maureeya, I see you are now wearing our traditional dress!" he cried, surveying the long loose pants and tunic I'd bought in Allahabad, and changed into inside the tent. "Your husband must wear a dhoti! He would look in the mirror and instantly be restored in his self-esteem! The dhoti is suiting tall men like your husband. Even I, a dwarf, am feeling so happy when I see myself in a dhoti."

He took us to a small, gloomy shop owned by one of his friends, where he selected a length of fine white cotton and showed Dag how to wrap it around his waist and loop it between his legs.

"Mr. Dag and Maureeya, now you are a fine couple!" he pronounced. "And please tell me: is your marriage love marriage?"

We spent most of the afternoon in Tilak's chai shop. Squatting on his oven, he watched us like a hawk, descending upon us to refill our teacups and our banana leaf plates, crying "Eat! Eat!" and standing over us with a maniacal expression on his face until we passed verdict on the food. When we insisted on paying for all we had, he took the money in a growling fashion.

We were joined in the chai shop by a varied array of fellow customers. Three saddhus came in first, and paid homage to the framed pictures of Hindu gods on the roughly plastered wall, hanging garlands around them and flicking them with Ganga water. Settling down on the long wooden bench beneath the pictures, they accepted Tilak's food and drink offerings and then turned to the serious business of smoking ganja. A toothless old village man arrived next, followed by a local dairy farmer with milk for sale in the two buckets suspended from a plank across his shoulders. Finally a suave young man called Pradip came in. He wore Western clothes, said he was from Varanasi and claimed to be India's break-dancing champion.

"Michael Jackson is my guru," he told me. "He had operation to make him white. Very beautiful now."

Dag was attempting a conversation in Hindi with the old man and the dairy farmer. *"Janver doktar,"* he was saying. "Animal doctor."

The dairy farmer was excitedly waggling his head, while the old man pulled at Dag's dhoti, asking *"Kitna? Kitna?"* "How much?"

"Ek sau rupees," Dag told him. "One hundred rupees."

This information stopped the conversation. Tilak descended from his perch on the oven, the saddhus laid down their chillums and everyone gathered around to examine Dag's dhoti.

"Bahut mehenga!" "Too much!" cried the old man, and he hurried out of the chai shop.

Tilak remounted his perch looking intensely worried, no doubt anticipating the storm about to break.

"Your husband was cheated," explained Pradip with a bored sigh. "This dhoti is farmer standard, worth no more than fifty rupees."

When the old man reappeared with Sudraj in tow, everyone jumped to their feet, and chaos ensued. One of the saddhus declared Sudraj to be an honest man, another accused him of being in league with the dhoti-seller, the old man shook his staff in Sudraj's face, Sudraj imploringly bleated, "Mr. Dag, Maureeya, I am not a cheating man!" The saddhus began arguing with each other, the dairy farmer tried to soothe them, and Tilak squatted on the counter, scratching his belly and giving passersby the "tension" signal, wrapping his second finger over his index finger. After half an hour of this, with no apparent resolution, Sudraj slunk out of the chai shop and everyone else calmed down.

"It has been agree," said Pradip.

"What has been agree?" we asked.

"The problem is over," he insisted, wafting his hand about as if to remove a bad smell. "Now, please be telling me, is it true, as I see on the television, that in America some people are starving themselves to death while others are eating themselves to death?"

"Quite true," I told him.

"And this dairy farmer wishes you to tell him if it is true that in America people are eating cows?"

"I'm afraid so."

He relayed this fact to the dairy farmer, who shook his head in dismay.

After evening puja, Dag set up our camp stove on top of the courtyard wall and began preparing dhal. The villagers who gathered to watch were at first relieved to learn that we were not eating meat, like our friends in America, then horrified to realize that Dag was cooking while his wife relaxed. Enjoying the attention, Dag put on quite a show, giving the men an impromptu cookery lesson and sharing with them his secret ingredient of a spot of sugar added to the lentils. We'd now been awake for over forty hours, so as soon as we'd eaten I went straight to bed. When I was in my sleeping bag, I unzipped the tent window. Through the screen I could see our kayak, and the goat curled up against it, scratching its head on the prow. Some musicians had joined Dag on the temple steps. They played haunting rhythms on tabla, harmonium and hand bells, and sang slow, sad songs. Pleasantly lulled, I drifted off toward sleep.

But not for long. A dazzling light shone full on my face, then traced around the inside of the tent. Shielding my eyes, I peered out to see Tilak hunkered down by the tent door, and four or five men bending down to peer in at me over his shoulder.

"English," one of them said. "Plastic."

Tilak grinned at me, and again shone the light into my face.

"*Nind!*" I said firmly—"Sleep!"—and to clarify the point I zipped up the window.

The men had a brief conference and left, but minutes later I heard approaching footsteps, and the tent began shaking violently.

"Maureeya? Maureeya?"

"Sudraj," I hissed. "Please go away, I am very tired."

Another flashlight beamed through the nylon walls. "Maureeya! Hello! Come on! Music! Tabla!"

It carried on—footsteps, shaking, flashlights, insistent voices, until, in desperation, I took a sleeping tablet and finally escaped into sleep.

At 4 A.M. the goat got up and peed against the side of our tent. Then someone began noisily sweeping up the courtyard, including right around the base of the tent. The clanking, squeaking and muttering that started up next turned out to be people stopping to fill up their chembus from the temple pump before heading to the toilet areas along the riverbank. Still bleary from the sleeping tablet, I forced myself out of bed and down the hill toward the women's toilet area, anxious to take advantage of the privacy of darkness. When I returned to bed I fell into a deep, blissful sleep—until 6 a.m., when a deafening clanging of bells announced the beginning of morning puja.

During the next three days, the temple steps became a village clinic as news of Dag's first-aid skills spread. He treated burns and ulcerated wounds, and gave away most of our medicines to remedy anything he could diagnose. On our last afternoon, the clinic was joined by a wedding party. We offered to move our campsite for the occasion, but no one would hear of it. Sackcloth was spread over the stone flags of the courtyard for the guests to sit on, and the ceremony went on around our tent and kayak. The bride was completely wrapped up in a golden cloth, so that even her face was hidden. A pujari with a dramatic Salvador Dali mustache led her and the groom through a series of pujas. Coconuts were broken, rice scattered, sandalwood smeared, incense burned. The groom tied a cloth to the bride's sari, slung the cloth over his shoulder and walked several times around the temple while she stumbled along behind him, loudly weeping and supported by her female relatives. The couple were then knotted together with the cloth and taken over to pray by a sacred fire burning in a corner of the courtyard. By now several of the guests had lost interest in the wedding. Some were clustered around our kayak, minutely examining it; others had joined me on the steps and were peering over my shoulder at the notes I was taking. Dogs were lolling about, the goat was chomping its way through one corner of the sackcloth, and pilgrims arriving at the temple were getting muddled up with the wedding party. Wanting to escape the heat of the afternoon, we wandered off to Tilak's chai shop for tea and a chat. As we left, the bride was being led into the Sitala shrine, and the weary groom was sitting next to our tent, surrounded by women who were smearing his face with milk curds.

An hour or so later, shouts, screams and wails coming from the direction of the temple brought us to our feet.

"*Aram, aram,*" said Tilak. "Relax".

He flapped his hands to gesture that we should sit down. A huddle of people hurried past, clutching in its midst a gold-wrapped figure. Some wedding guests ran by next, shouting news of the scandal to Tilak as they went. Down at the temple, the groom's family had complained that the bride's dowry was too meager, and had demanded an extra 4,000 rupees. When this wasn't forthcoming, a fight had broken out and the couple had been separated and dragged off in opposite directions by their respective families.

"It happens every time," Tilak told us as he nonchalantly stoked the fire in his oven. "By nightfall it will all be settled."

That evening we were invited to eat with a hollow-faced man called Ramcharan, who was a poor Brahmin and a pujari. We sat cross-legged with him on a wooden table in his courtyard. The place was spotlessly clean, and Ramcharan was dressed in bright white kurta and pants. Food was served to us by his eldest son on stainless steel trays. The spinach and potato sabzee was delicious, but the dhal was strangely sweet—news of Dag's recipe had obviously spread and been exaggerated. At the end of the meal, we were served with bowls of warm buffalo milk, and a dish containing some sugar. There was no spoon to add the sugar—as usual we'd eaten with our hands. Ramcharan came to the rescue: looking me straight in the eye, with his right hand he scooped up some sugar and dropped it into my bowl, then stuck his fingers in the warm milk and waggled them around until the sugar dissolved. Graciously, I thanked him and lifted the bowl to my lips, while next to me Dag suffered a sudden, and unconvincing, fit of coughing.

Because this was a Brahmin family, the kitchen was at the back of the house, safely out of sight of the defiling eyes of lower-caste visitors. I'd only once got a glimpse of Ramcharan's wife when she peeked around a door, her face covered by her sari. But after the meal I was taken into the kitchen to meet her. I went through a small room filled with three charpois, ducked under a low doorway, and stepped into the kitchen. It had a ceiling of split bamboo, and in one corner mud steps led up to the attic, where wood was stored for fuel. Bala Devi sat behind a low mud wall, next to an adobe oven and a neat array of brass pots and spoons. She was dressed in a simple cotton sari, and had buck teeth and a betel-stained smile. She laid down some sackcloth for me to sit on, fetched a bowl of oil and began massaging my feet and calves. The plastic bangles around her wrists rattled as she forcefully kneaded my muscles. This was an honor usually accorded to elderly women. News of my age and childlessness had spread like wildfire around the village, and before we left their house, Ramcharan and Bala Devi made a puja to the statue of Goddess Sitala in one of their wall niches, asking that I should be granted a son.

After four days, we had to tear ourselves away from Sultanpur. It took hours to say good-bye to everyone. Our parting with Tilak was typically brusque.

"In Varanasi," he yelled, poking Dag in the chest, "no ganja! Poison! No chai! Poison! No guide! Robber!"

Assuring Tilak that we would remember this advice, and thanking him for his kindness, we headed to the ghats for our last bathe in the Ganga.

As I stood waist deep in water, a woman teasingly splashed me like a buffalo. The debris of pujas littered the surface, and a little upstream of me a man cleared his throat and spat out the contents. Impassively, I watched the glob of green sputum float by. Then I held my nose and ducked beneath the water.

We sat in the kayak while Ramcharan did a final puja with us. He tied new strings around our wrists, rubbed our foreheads with sandalwood paste, sprinkled us with coconut milk. Six weeks ago, in Hardwar, I'd participated in the same ritual with a cool detachment. Now, as I watched our banana-leaf boats bob away downstream, their little camphor flames brightly burning, I found myself silently thanking Holy Mother Ganga for our safe passage along her.

Field after field of orange marigolds slipped by. Ahead, tiers of curlicued ashrams, temples and palaces rose up, stretching away for miles and fading into a brown-gold haze. We were approaching Varanasi, the City of Light, the holiest place along the Ganga, the most auspicious place for a Hindu to die. We pulled down our sail, put our paddles away, and let the current take us. The ghats seemed to go on forever: ghats where pujaris sat beneath large sun umbrellas, ghats where bathers undressed in open-fronted wooden cubicles, burning ghats where buffalo chewed on piles of wood fifteen feet high and where assembly lines of funeral pyres crackled side by side; submerged ghats where the onion domes of collapsed temples emerged from the water, ghats where Western sannyasins bathed, ghats from where Japanese tourists videoed us. We drifted by them all, until the stone ghats ended and were replaced by muddy banks leading up to dilapidated buildings four stories high, with narrow, dank lanes running between them. Just before a railway bridge we pulled ashore, and were quickly surrounded by a group of louche characters in ragged lungis and shirts, who greedily eyed our boat and its contents. We took out the prasad we'd brought from our puja in Sultanpur—sweets and pieces of coconut—and handed it around. Instantly, the mood changed. The men touched the prasad to their foreheads, smiled at us with blackened, broken teeth, and then helped Dag take the boat apart.

Two days later, in our air-conditioned room in the New Delhi Maurya Sheraton's Executive Suite, I unpacked the bag containing our grubby clothes and blankets. Fine sand, flecked with glittering mica chips, showered onto the thick carpet, and then some small, hard, black balls rolled out. I called Dag over, and we knelt down to peer at the holy goat's droppings. There was a knock at the door, the room service boy came in and stepped carefully around us, bearing a tray with a silver teapot and china cups. As I stood to sign the bill, I thought of Tilak brewing up chai over his adobe oven, of Bala Devi smearing dung over her kitchen floor, and of Ramcharan, walking along the lanes of Sultanpur on his way to the temple—400 miles and several light years away.

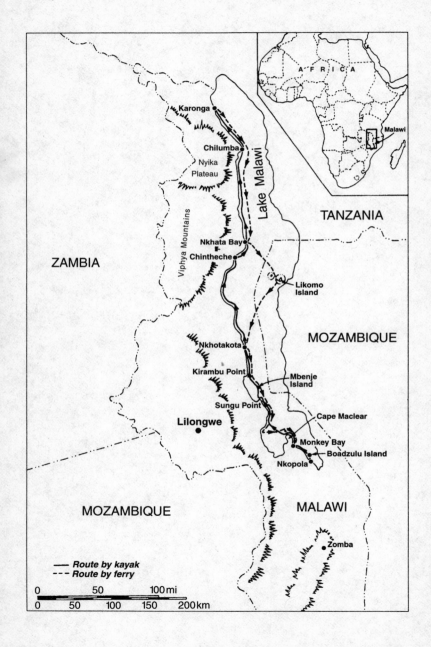

AFRICA

Malawi

Karonga

Chilumba

Nyika
Plateau

Lake Malawi

TANZANIA

Viphya Mountains

ZAMBIA

Nkhata Bay
Chintheche

Likomo
Island

MOZAMBIQUE

Nkhotakota

Kirambu Point

Mbenje
Island

Sungu Point

Cape Maclear

Lilongwe

Monkey Bay

Boadzulu Island

Nkopola

MOZAMBIQUE

MALAWI

Zomba

—— Route by kayak
- - - Route by ferry

0   50   100 mi
0   50   100   150   200 km